Why should anyone be led by you?

Why should anyone be led by you?

WHAT IT TAKES TO BE AN AUTHENTIC LEADER

Rob Goffee / Gareth Jones

HARVARD BUSINESS REVIEW PRESS

Boston, Massachusetts

Library of Congress Cataloging-in-Publication Data

Goffee, Robert.
    Why should anyone be led by you? : what it takes to be an authentic leader :
  with a new preface by the authors / Rob Goffee and Gareth Jones.
    pages   cm
    Previous edition: 2006.
    ISBN 978-1-63369-108-7 (alk. paper)
    1. Leadership.   I. Jones, Gareth, 1951 August 21–   II. Title.
  HD57.7.G663   2015
    658.4'092—dc23   2015017951

ISBN: 9781633691087
eISBN: 9784633691094

*This book is dedicated to
all those who strive to
lead organizations.*

CONTENTS

Since this book was first published, the world has experienced some significant shocks. Most obviously, the 2008 financial crisis—the biggest crisis of capitalism since 1929. The fall of Lehman Brothers and the rapid spread of financial disorder threatened the entire global economic system. The impact on businesses—small, medium, and large—has been huge. And the public sector has not been immune, either. Geopolitical change has been significant. Even as we write this, both the short- and long-term future of the Middle East seem highly uncertain. In Europe we have witnessed the rebirth of Russian territorial ambitions just as the Eurozone threatens to fall into stagflation.

Do these dramatic changes make the question "Why should anyone be led by you?" more or less relevant? Our answer is unequivocal. The need for authentic leadership is more pressing than ever. When the economic history of the global financial crisis is finally written, we will see that brave leadership on the part of political figures on both sides of the Atlantic prevented a significant recession from becoming another Great Depression. In the corporate world, great leaders have begun the process of leading us to sustained growth and continuing innovation. The world needs great organizations—and great leaders—more than ever. As for Europe and the Middle East, we await the emergence of brave and visionary leaders who can positively transform a volatile and dangerous situation.

So we are confident that the key messages of this book still resonate. In fact, the emergence of the knowledge economy has made leadership both more important and more difficult. The clever people who inhabit the knowledge economy do not, for the most part, want to be leaders—and many of them don't want to be led! They want to be left alone to pursue their personal goals and the Next Big Thing. Yet they are significantly more productive when they are well led. We addressed this issue in our book *Clever: Leading Your Smartest, Most Creative People.*

Since this book's original publication, it's fair to say that the concept of "authentic leadership" has become a modern orthodoxy. Cynics might even conclude that authenticity has become an industry. We are, however, still convinced that authenticity, as defined in this book, differs significantly from its interpretation by others. Our argument was—and remains—that authenticity manifests itself in context and in relationships with others. It is never solely an attribute of individuals. That's what our central theme "Be yourself—more—with skill" really means. Our book is infused with a sociological perspective, in contrast to the predominantly psychological approach taken in many accounts of authenticity.

The pressures on leaders have become greater. They have less time than they used to. They need to assess situations (a key skill, called *situation sensing,* we discuss in this book) more quickly. This means they must read context and think about how to redefine it faster. If they don't, social media will redefine it for them. In addition, the organizational world is increasingly characterized by geographically dispersed, often virtual teams. Leaders must achieve closeness in imaginative ways. They must identify and take advantage of cultural differences using new forms of communication. All of these changes reinforce rather than undermine the key leadership skills we discuss in this book.

Despite this concern with speed, we stress in the book that leadership development is a continuous process. Great leaders are never finished. All of us are challenged to constantly review and renew our leadership skills. Again, this is not an entirely individual task. Effective leadership development is fueled by honest, authentic conversations with others. And honesty, in many organizations, is in short supply. We address this particular challenge—how to create authentic workplaces and organizations—in our new book *Why Should Anyone Work Here?*

As we have talked about our ideas with many people in diverse organizations, we have urged them to find others with whom they can have honest discussions about the true nature of leadership. Our ambition is that this book will provide the questions that fuel those discussions.

The big question remains: Why should anyone be led by you?

Why Should Anyone Be Led by You?

AT THE BEGINNING of the new millennium, our research was driven by this single, simple question. It had an impact. Audiences we addressed throughout the world paused for thought when they were asked it. Rooms fell silent as people pondered their right to lead and the willingness of their followers to be led by them. A *Harvard Business Review* article with the question as its title produced a flood of communication.

Over the last five years, the question has taken us in intriguing, exciting, and often perplexing directions. Along the way, we have interviewed dozens of leaders (and their followers) in the corporate world and beyond—in schools, hospitals, sports organizations, and elsewhere.[1] After all, leadership is all-embracing. It is not the sole preserve of high-profile CEOs. As we have continued to work with students and consulting clients, we have learned even more.

This is a book whose genesis was driven by a question, but it is one whose fruition, we hope, provides a range of answers to the leadership riddles and dilemmas we now face—as well as an entirely new range of questions.

Our own work on leadership began some twenty-five years ago and has followed three paths. First, as academics, we exhaustively surveyed the leadership research of the past century before developing our own working model. Second, as consultants, we tested our approach with managers and leaders in workshops worldwide and through observations with scores of clients. And third, as leaders, we vetted our ideas in our own organizations.

Throughout, the focus of our research has been on leaders who excel at inspiring people—leaders who succeed in capturing hearts, minds, and souls. We are fascinated by leadership that, reaching back to the ideas of Max Weber, is antibureaucratic and charismatic. To have leaders with these qualities is not everything in business, but our contention is that it is worth a substantial amount. Indeed, great results are likely to be impossible without it.

Make no mistake: leadership is about results. Great leadership has the potential to excite people to extraordinary levels of achievement. But it is not only about performance; it is also about meaning. This is an important point—and one that is often overlooked by contemporary leadership literature. Leaders at all levels make a difference to performance. They do so because they make performance meaningful.

It is to state the obvious that the impact of leadership on our lives is profound—at work, in our spiritual lives, in sport, and of course, in politics. But this observation does capture a peculiarly modern obsession: the search for authentic leaders. In Western societies, at least, there is a deep and deepening disenchantment with the able role player or, worse still, the skilled apparatchik—of the political or corporate kind. We are increasingly suspicious that we are being "worked." The search for authenticity is ever more pressing.

The Authentic Quest

There is evidence of the desire for authenticity all around us in popular culture. The seemingly inexorable rise of reality TV (a truly Orwellian phrase as participants are manipulated for an anonymous and isolated audience of voyeurs) is one manifestation. Or we can watch soap operas portraying a nostalgic view of communities— filling the gap left by the decline in genuinely communal life painstakingly dissected in Robert Putnam's *Bowling Alone*.[2]

These questions about authenticity are related to a wider set of concerns about how we live now. Critics of modern societies persistently point to three concerns that, in their view, restrict or prevent the authentic expression of humanity and make it harder to be yourself.

To begin with, there is the triumph of individualism. If there is one overriding characteristic of the modern era, it is the extension of personal freedom through the march of individualism. At the heart of this, of course, lies a paradox. While few would deny that modern life has increased the scope for human choice, many have cautioned against the rise of excessive individualism: a world characterized not by the authentic expression of self but as simply selfish.

At its core, this critique argues that authenticity itself rests upon some sense of moral regulation. We cannot be freely ourselves without an overarching set of shared moral values. In their absence we get not authentic leaders but narcissistic ones. The damaging scandals at Enron, Tyco, Hollinger International, and WorldCom add contemporary bite to this critique.

Closely related to this lack of moral regulation is the Weberian notion of the modern world dominated by a particular way of thinking. Weber calls this "technical rationality."[3] In more modern terminology, this is often called *instrumental reason*: the rationality of an act is judged by the connection between means and ends, where the ends are given. It is a view of rationality stripped of morality. Whatever your problem, there is a technically rational solution to it.

For Max Weber, the triumph of this way of thinking constitutes the nightmare of modern life. He writes passionately of mankind trapped in an iron cage—from which it cannot escape. This critique of modern life had been elaborated many times, but of special relevance for us are its consequences in the workplace.

From this perspective, work is degraded. It becomes the means to the satisfaction of other ends—paying the mortgage, buying designer-label goods—rather than being a milieu both for the building and discovery of an authentic self and for its disclosure. Both workers and executives are just another kind of *input* to be downsized, delayered, and discarded. Our workplaces become not arenas for the expression of authenticity but soulless machines for the production of conformity. This is a theme captured in the grim pessimism of Kafka's novels and railed against in the long line of antibureaucratic heroes Western culture has produced, from Charlie Chaplin in *Modern Times* to Yossarian in *Catch-22* via *The Good Soldier Schweik* in Jaroslav Hasek's novel: all human beings who resist being processed.

One final theme helps to explain our focus on authenticity. It is most eloquently articulated in the work of Alexis de Tocqueville, who fears the rise of "soft" despotism—a society in which individuals decline to engage in acts of self-government in exchange for a government that meets their material needs.[4] He fears the withering of civil society—the myriad of informal associations that both provide social glue and critically function as vehicles for the expression of self.

This Tocqueville theme finds later expression in David Reisman's classic *The Lonely Crowd*: a picture of isolated, atomized individuals lacking the social relationships from which they could create an authentic self.[5] A similar anxiety is unearthed in Putnam's *Bowling Alone*.[6] Putnam produces a veritable barrage of evidence to support this claim: declining membership of parent-teacher associations, falling attendance at public meetings, and of course, despite the popularity of bowling, the collapse of the bowling leagues.

All of these arguments help to explain the contemporary focus on authenticity. It is a reaction to the turbulence and change of modern life. Work and family institutions seem under threat. Recent geopolitical events have dramatically and tragically reinforced this sense of turbulence. As rates of change increase, individuals are ever more motivated to search for constancy and meaning. We've become increasingly suspicious of a world dominated by the mere role player.

Authenticity at Work

In organizations, the search for the meaning and cohesion leaders provide has become especially acute. The traditional sources of organizational cohesion have all become weaker. The old world was characterized by elaborate hierarchies, by more or less stable careers (for some, never for all), and by clear boundaries between organizations. All this has changed. Now hierarchies in most organizations are becoming flatter, driven by the need for faster response times and by the competitive pressure to drive down costs. But hierarchies were not just structural coordinating devices in organizations. Rather, and much more significantly, they were sources of meaning. It is not that long ago that after fifteen years you had made it to deputy assistant to the superintendent—and you had done well. As hierarchies flatten, meaning disappears. We look to leadership to instill our organizations with meaning.[7]

Equally significant is the changing shape of careers. Not so long ago, the psychological contract for many (but never for all) involved movement up a relatively stable career ladder, often with one organization. Those days are gone. Instead, individuals maximize their life opportunities through increasing their human capital, knowing that their organizations can offer little certainty for the future. Part of this is liberating—individuals as architects of their own working lives—but part is the removal of another source of meaning at work.

Even organizational boundaries have begun to break down. The old theory of firm behavior described discrete organizations competing in more or less perfect markets, where some won and some lost. Today organizations make alliances with suppliers, customers, and sometimes competitors. The organization man, with company blood coursing through his veins, has to come to terms with a world of high ambiguity in which overidentification with one organization is a problem rather than a career.[8]

Finally, the spate of corporate scandals at Enron et al. produced a huge loss of faith in our corporate leaders. If there is one good outcome here, it is that we may be finally cured of the cult of the heroic CEO. There is, for example, a growing interest in so-called quiet leaders. Our concern is that in time this, too, could become a leadership cul-de-sac. We do not want leadership clones—noisy or quiet. We want real leaders.

The corporate scandals are a symptom of amoral leadership. The damage done to the ideology that makes our economic system cohere has been substantial. The cozy belief that capitalist enterprises are led in the interests of stakeholders has taken a battering. There is widespread cynicism about the state of our political economy.

Executives are not immune to this. Interviewed at work about what gives their lives meaning, they mouth the latest corporate propaganda: "increasing shareholder value," "delighting customers." Asked the same questions at home, they admit to profound symptoms of meaninglessness as they struggle with work-related stress and dysfunctional family lives. We face an epidemic of anomie.[9]

It seems that Max Weber's grim predictions of the "disenchantment of the world" may be fulfilled.[10]

All of this has left modern societies with a profound moral vacuum. We are not sure what we believe in. Indeed, one notable contemporary social phenomenon in the Western world is the growth of cult religions as people struggle to find something to believe in.

The demand for authentic leadership is there and growing. As traditional hierarchies disintegrate, only leadership can fill the void. Without a clearly articulated purpose, meaning is elusive. Leadership provides that articulation. This search for authenticity and leadership is reinforced whenever we work inside organizations. CEOs tell us that their most pressing need is for more leaders in their organizations—not the consummate role players who seem to surround them. And lower down the organization, the plea is either for more inspiring leadership or, just as common, a fierce desire to develop leadership skills for themselves. Authentic leadership has become the most prized organizational and individual asset.

ONE

Be Yourself—
More—with Skill

WHEN WE ASK PEOPLE in organizations—executives, first-line supervisors, head teachers, hospital nurses—which set of competences they would most like to develop, all provide the same answer: help us to become more effective leaders. They have seen that leadership makes a big difference to their lives and the performance of their organizations.

Equally, when we ask CEOs what is the biggest problem they face, they unerringly reply: our organizations need more leaders at every level.

So, given the hunger for leadership, why are leaders in such short supply? We think there are two fundamental reasons:

First, organizations desire leaders but structure themselves in ways that kill leadership. Far too many of our organizations—in business, in the public sector, and in the not-for-profit sector—are machines for the destruction of leadership. They encourage either conformists or role players with an impoverished sense of who they are and what they stand for. Neither makes for effective leaders. And of course, this gives rise to legions of disenchanted followers, producing the deepest organizational malaise of modern times: cynicism.

Second, our understanding of leadership is blinkered. Having reviewed much of the existing leadership literature, both new and old, we find it surprising how little we know.[1] This observation is not a criticism of our academic colleagues who, no doubt, like us, have pondered long and hard on the mysteries of leadership. Rather, it is an observation about the methods we have used and the fundamental assumptions upon which much of the research has rested.

The main body of leadership literature focuses on the *characteristics* of leaders. This gives it a strong psychological bias. It sees leadership qualities as inherent to the individual. The underlying assumption is that leadership is something we do *to* other people. But in our view, leadership should be seen as something we do *with* other people. Leadership must always be viewed as a relationship between the leader and the led.

Books on leadership persistently try to find a recipe for leadership. Beleaguered executives are invited to compare themselves with lists of leadership competences and characteristics—against which they always find themselves wanting. Attempts to imitate others, even the most successful leaders, are doomed to failure. As Bill Burns, CEO of the $16 billion global pharmaceutical division of F. Hoffmann-La Roche Ltd. (Roche) told us, "The idea of us all becoming Jack Welch is nonsense."[2]

In our view, there are no universal leadership characteristics. What works for one leader will not work for another. We think that those aspiring to leadership need to discover what it is about themselves that they can mobilize in a leadership context. They need to identify and deploy their own personal leadership assets.[3]

Our position is different from much contemporary thinking. This insists that effective leadership rests upon full self-knowledge. This sometimes leads to excessive concern with the inner drives of the leader and finds expression in some formulations of emotional intelligence (EI) and more broadly in the psychoanalytic literature on leadership.[4] No doubt EI is a highly useful life skill, but our observations of leaders suggest that few develop full self-knowledge. Rather, our experience suggests that effective leaders have an overarching sense of purpose together with *sufficient* self-knowledge of their potential leadership assets. They don't know it all, but they know *enough*.

Against this backdrop of increasing demand for leadership, an organizational predisposition to kill leadership, and an inadequate understanding of what leadership entails and requires, the key question is:

How Can We Become More Effective As Leaders and As Developers of Leaders?

The answer, we believe, lies in an explicit recognition of three fundamental axioms about leadership.

Situational

First, leadership is *situational*. What is required of the leader will always be influenced by the situation. This is commonsensical, but true.[5]

History is full of examples of leaders who found their time and place, but whose qualities lost their appeal when things moved on. Winston Churchill, for example, was an inspirational wartime leader, but his bulldog style was ill suited to the reconstruction agenda of postwar Britain. Similarly, George Bush (senior) had a colossal opinion-poll lead in the immediate aftermath of the first Iraq war, and yet in the following year he lost to Bill Clinton. By contrast, Nelson Mandela's ability to offer leadership across widely differing contexts exemplifies situational adjustment from a prison cell on Robben Island to the graceful lawns of Union House in Pretoria.

There are parallels in organizational life. For example, some hard-edged, cost-cutting turnaround managers are unable to offer leadership when there is a need to build. But their more adaptable colleagues adjust to shifting agendas—and carry their teams with them.

As we will see, the ability to observe and understand existing situations, something we call *situation sensing,* is key to leadership. This involves a mixture of sensory and cognitive abilities. Effective leaders pick up important situational signals. They are able to tune in to the organizational frequency to understand what is going on beneath the surface. This is both a micro and a macro skill, visible in daily routine encounters (meetings, walking the corridors, elevator conversations) as well as in big, strategic decisions (Does this acquisition smell right? Are these good people to partner with?). Skillful leaders are then able to adjust appropriately, self-consciously deploying their personal capabilities, or leadership assets.

We do not mean to be excessively deterministic in our claim that leadership is situational. The situation, or context, the leader inherits is simply the starting point. Clearly, leaders' actions themselves help to shape the context, altering the initial situation they found. In so doing, they are able to impact—and therefore reshape—the situations within which they lead. Through their inter-actions, effective leaders construct *alternative contexts* to those which they initially inherited. They use their personal leadership assets to reframe situations—to the benefit of those they lead. This last point is important. It is not sufficient for leaders to reframe a situation to their own advantage; true leadership requires reframing for the benefit of the followers. That is the basis on which the relationship is founded.

Nonhierarchical

This leads to our second observation: leadership is *nonhierarchical*. Much of the leadership literature is overly concerned with those who reach the top of organizations. In fact, we would go so far as to say that the persistent misconception that people who occupy senior organizational positions are leaders has probably damaged our capacity to understand leadership more than anything else. It has blinded us to the true nature of leadership.

While we recognize that there is a relationship between hierarchy and leadership (they may fulfill a similar function, for example, by investing authority), we view the relationship as contingent. Being given a particular organizational title—team leader, section head, and vice president—may confer some hierarchical authority, but it certainly does not make you a leader. Hierarchy alone is neither a necessary nor a sufficient condition for the exercise of leadership.

Indeed, it could be argued that the qualities that take you to the top of large-scale and often highly political organizations are not obviously the ones associated with leadership. People who make it to the top do so for a whole variety of reasons—including political acumen, personal ambition, time-serving, even nepotism—rather than real leadership quality.

Our interviews and experience inside organizations confirms that leadership is not the sole preserve of the chosen few. Great organizations have leaders at all levels. Some of the first work we did on leadership involved examining military organizations. Our assumption was that their hierarchical nature would make leadership development difficult. Nothing could be further from the truth. The best military organizations understand that when they move into action, they simply cannot rely on hierarchy; it may be obliterated when the first mortar lands. It is imperative that they develop leadership capability throughout. They do.

It is not just the military that has reached this realization. Consider Sonae, Portugal's largest company, an organization we will examine in more detail later. Sonae's business stretches from wood veneers to telecommunications, taking in a huge retail operation. It focuses relentlessly on high performance—mediocrity is not tolerated. The company's mission statement starkly states, "At Sonae you are either a leader or a candidate to be a leader." The implication is clear; if you are neither, Sonae is not the place for you.

Successful organizations—be they hospitals, charities, or commercial enterprises—seek to build leadership capability widely and to give people the opportunity to exercise it.

Relational

The third foundation of our view of leadership is that leadership is *relational*. Put simply, you cannot be a leader without followers. Much of early trait theory seemed to ignore this. By trying to distill the characteristics of leaders, it neglected the fact that leadership is a relationship built actively by both parties. In reality, leadership is always a social construct that is re-created by the relationships between leaders and those they aspire to lead. Effective leaders are not simply amalgams of desirable traits; they are

actively and reciprocally engaged in a complex series of relationships that require cultivation and nurture. Like all social creations,
this web of relationships is fragile and requires constant re-creation.[6]
You can confirm this every time you talk to a successful CEO, a
sports coach, or a team leader. All will tell you that much of their
leadership effort is devoted to the maintenance of particular kinds
of relationships with their followers.

This insistence on the relational nature of leadership does not
mean that these relationships are necessarily harmonious—they
may well be edgy—but they are about leaders knowing how to
excite followers to become great performers.

Does this mean generalizations are impossible? We don't think
so. Some fundamental principles of leadership do apply across the
board. Followers want feelings of excitement and personal significance from their leaders—something confirmed by research.[7] In
addition, they wish to feel part of something bigger—a community,
if you will. But above all, they look for leaders who are authentic.
Indeed, authenticity is integral to the relationship. Without it, there
can be no significant investment of trust on either side.

How leaders demonstrate authenticity—and how followers sense
it—is a complex theme to which we return at many points in this
book. For now, it is sufficient to note that, although this will involve
different behaviors in different contexts, effective leaders are still
able to communicate a consistent sense of self that is invested—
skillfully—in each of the roles that they play.

Making Sense of Authenticity

The concept of authenticity has been extensively discussed
from a psychological and psychoanalytic perspective. Much of this
literature focuses on the complex, maybe endless, process of self-

discovery.[8] From that rich seam of research we take three critical elements.

First, authentic leaders display a *consistency between words and deeds*. Leaders who do what they say—who practice what they preach—are more likely seen as "genuine" and therefore authentic. Nothing betrays the aspiring leader quite so much as the attempt to persuade others to do things that they would never do themselves. But an ability to do what you say is not enough on its own.

The second element of authentic leadership is the capacity to display *coherence in role performances*. In other words, despite the unavoidable need to play different roles at different times for different audiences, authentic leaders *communicate a consistent underlying thread*. They display a "real self" that holds these separate performances together.

Closely linked to this is the third and final element. Authentic leadership involves a kind of *comfort with self*, which is perhaps the hardest aspect of all to attain. This is the internal source from which consistency of role performance is drawn. The *Concise Oxford Dictionary* defines that which is authentic as having "undisputed origins."[9] And in a leadership context, this is what followers are looking for: a set of performances that have a common origin.

The first two of these three elements have received considerable attention. The distinction between espoused and enacted values was first drawn many years ago by Harvard Business School's Chris Argyris.[10] It has been most recently revisited with a new twist in Jeffrey Pfeffer's discussion of the "knowing-doing" gap.[11] Coherence in role performances through the "invention of self" is a recurring theme subtly explored in the extensive work of Warren Bennis.[12]

Comfort with self, the third theme, relates to the interplay between personal origins and destinations. It is less widely discussed in the leadership literature but connects with a rich tradition in sociology.[13]

Yet, despite the intense work of many scholars, these insights have remained largely unexplored in understanding the significance of authenticity as it defines the relationship between leaders and followers. In the last five years, there has been a real interest in authenticity as a property of the leader.[14] However, there has been little discussion of authenticity as enacted in social relationships.

So what does all this mean for those who aspire to leadership?

The simple answer (deceptively simple) is that to be a more effective leader, you must *be yourself—more—with skill*.

Me Myself

First, to be a leader, you must *be yourself*. This is our theme in the opening chapters of the book. Followers want to be led by a person, not a role holder or a position filler or a bureaucrat. Inevitably, then, the central question—explicitly or implicitly—in the mind of others who might follow us is, "What is different about you that equips you to lead?" Or, to put it another way, "What is special about you that means I should follow you?"

But this does not take us back to trait theory, which largely failed in its attempts to find *patterned* differences. What correlations there are in trait-based research are weak. For example, effective leaders are often shown to have slightly above-average levels of confidence. The point to note is *slightly* above average—and that the causal relationship remains indeterminate. In other words, it is at least plausible that their self-confidence arises from gradual exposure to successful leadership experiences. Despite great endeavors, trait theory has never conclusively established cause and effect.

Our own view is almost the polar opposite of trait theory. We argue that effective leaders know those individual differences that might help them in a leadership role—*whatever they might be*—and use them to their advantage. They must identify differences that have meaning for followers. Think, for example, of the way in which Sir Richard Branson, the Virgin boss, is able to use his physical appearance—casual dress, long hair, and a beard—to convey the informality and nonconformity that has become a central part of his leadership and, indeed, the Virgin brand.

This is an example of an individual skillfully deploying his differences in ways that attract followers. In this case, the differences are significant, real, and perceived. By this we mean that Branson's differences *signify* a message; they are *authentic*, not falsely manufactured; and they are *seen* by others. We are talking, then, not of *any* personal difference but of an artful and authentic display—often fine-tuned over many years—of genuine differences that have the potential to excite others.

Or consider this example. We met and observed a cleaning supervisor in a large New York office building. Marcia is a Puerto Rican American woman who leads a team of office cleaners. She is a larger-than-life character—in every sense. She is intensely proud of her origins and yet a subtle reader of the many cultures represented by her team. She can be brash—this *is* New York—but it's done in a knowing kind of way. Her language and clothes are exotic. She uses humor to devastating effect: woe betide the slovenly cleaner! Her passion is for the office workers to notice and comment favorably on the cleanliness of the offices. With all this, members of her team know that she cares about them and about getting the job done right. In unpromising circumstances, she has forged a high-performance team.

Marcia and Richard Branson have a lot in common. So how do they do it? As we noted, this does not rest upon complete or even deep self-knowledge. Rather, it is developed and honed pragmatically as leaders engage with their tasks and their followers. This is the difference, perhaps, between self-awareness and self-knowledge. Over time, these leaders figure out what works for them. The point is that they don't necessarily need to know why or how it works, as long as they can reproduce the effect. In fact, in our experience, this level of self-knowledge is more often absent.

In chapter 2, we explore how individuals come to know and deploy their differences, and we illustrate the impact this has on their followers. This journey of self-discovery has its roots in our origins—shaped as they are by such powerful forces as family, gender, locale, and social class. Effective leaders are able to extract from these experiences a sense of self that they are comfortable with despite, in many cases, a significant shift in their social milieu. They understand and are at ease with where they are in relation to where they started.

Showing yourself as a leader inevitably involves taking personal risks—and revealing weaknesses—and we deal with these themes in chapter 3. What is it that drives individuals to take personal risks? In our experience, it is an unbending sense of purpose. Great leaders *really* care—about an idea, values, a dream, or vision. It is this commitment that can carry them through adversity and personal risk. Think, for example, of the leaders of the civil rights movement who took enormous personal risks in pursuit of their dream.

Inevitably, as leaders expose themselves, they will always show us weaknesses as well as strengths. But does this make them less attractive as leaders? We think not. Clearly, demonstrating strengths lends leaders legitimacy—but not if weaknesses are denied. The desire to be led by a real person demands that we know something of a leader's human foibles and shortcomings. The claim of perfection will rarely convince us of another's humanity. And paradoxically, denying weakness is most likely to increase rather than reduce the leader's vulnerability.

The Context's the Thing

But although the link between self-knowledge and self-disclosure is a central—and increasingly fashionable—starting point for understanding effective leadership, it is not everything. The world is not that simple. Leadership does not take place in a vacuum: you must be yourself *in context*. Great leaders are able to read the context and respond accordingly. They tap into what exists and bring *more* to the party. In management jargon, they add value. This involves a subtle blend of authenticity and adaptation, of individuality and conformity. We discuss these capabilities in the middle chapters of the book.

In chapter 4, we discuss situation sensing. Using a complex mix of cognitive and observational skills, leaders pick up signals that help them explain what's happening without having others spell it out for them. These skills enable them to read and interpret the situation. They tune in so that they know when team morale is shaky or when complacency needs challenging. Often they appear to collect this information through osmosis. But although some individuals seem to have a natural instinct for sensing, we believe this skill can be learned and leaders can improve their sensing capabilities. In our work we have observed three powerful ways in which leaders have been able to hone their sensing abilities.

The first is early exposure to a range of different experiences. Sometimes this comes with a family background that involves mobility in childhood. This creates opportunities—and, perhaps, a need—for individuals to experience and make sense of different cultures and lifestyles.[15] On other occasions it arises from early career experiences that provide similar cultural contrasts across different occupational groups or business contexts. We have been struck, for example, by the number of leaders who, early in their careers, took on jobs at the edge of their organizations—typically selling—that brought them into contact with a range of different potential customers and incentivized them to get to know them better (to make the sale).

Take Franz Humer, the chief executive and chairman of the Roche pharmaceutical empire. Accomplished at detecting subtle shifts in ambience, he can read nuanced cues and sense unspoken opinions that elude less perceptive people. Humer told us that he developed his skill when he worked as a tour guide in his mid-twenties and was responsible for groups of one hundred or more. "There was no salary, only tips," he told us. "Pretty soon, I knew how to home in on particular groups. Eventually, I could predict within 10 percent how much I could earn from any particular group."

The second successful approach seems to be structured, experience-based learning where individuals are exposed to a range of direct experiences and helped to learn from them by skilled facilitators. Witness the remarkable growth of business school interpersonal skills programs, and 360-degree survey feedback. Both share the objective of encouraging individuals to sense better the situations they are in and the manner in which their behavior can impact them.

In one case, we interviewed a relatively lowly office manager in a large firm in Cincinnati. For him, a brief exposure to 360-degree feedback, delivered in a constructive and sympathetic manner, had proved a turning point in his leadership experiences.

The third approach—again increasingly popular among executives—is the use of a personal coach. Although coaching styles and methods vary, there is typically a shared ambition to create opportunities for individuals to practice skills in familiar and new situations and to receive feedback on their impact.

You do not need to be a senior executive in an organization to experience this coaching effect. Even better than coaches are good colleagues. We observed a relatively inexperienced young African American woman who was given the opportunity to lead the floor of a large retail outlet. Initially, she found the leadership aspects of the job rather daunting—most of the staff were older and more experienced than her. But she found and used a skilled mentor in one of the firm's buyers, and with gentle but persistent guidance, she blossomed into an exciting, even inspirational, leader.

But effective leaders do not simply react to context. They also shape it—by illuminating aspects of the situation that they can turn to their advantage. This theme is developed in chapter 4. It is further developed in chapter 5, where we argue that effective leaders conform *enough.*

This involves the skillful ability to communicate individuality, for collective benefit, in leadership roles. But it also involves an awareness of when and where to conform. Without this ability for measured conformity, leaders are unlikely to survive or make the connections they need to build successful relationships with others. Expressed differently, despite a clear sense of purpose and strong values, effective leaders seem to know where and when to make compromises. Think, for example, of the extent to which political leaders such as Nelson Mandela in South Africa, Gerry Adams in Northern Ireland,

and Senator George Mitchell in the Middle East have successfully "conformed enough" but always in pursuit of a clear set of values and political ideas. As a result, they have not lost their followers.

By conforming, they demonstrate common cause with their followers. Another way to think of this is in terms of consciously engaging an organizational gear. To be effective, the leader needs to ensure that his or her behaviors mesh sufficiently with the organizational culture to create traction. Leaders who fail to mesh will simply spin their wheels in isolation from their followers.

The central concept that informs this tension is what we call a sense of social realism.[16] This is an important part of being an authentic leader. In our experience, where individuals with leadership potential fail, it is most often because they are lacking an acute enough sense of social realism.

The Skill Factor

But knowing yourself and the context are not enough. You must also *act* as a leader. And since leadership is inevitably a relationship, we focus in the later chapters of the book on the leader's skill in managing relationships and communicating inspirationally and with good timing.

In chapter 6, we show how good leaders manage relationships by knowing when to be close—to empathize, to build relations of warmth, loyalty, and affection; and when to be distant—to keep people focused on the goal, to address poor performance, to give relationships an edge. Crucially, leaders are able to create this distance without resorting to formal hierarchy. To some extent, our discussion echoes the work of the early style theorists. But the fundamental concept underlying this tension—originally developed by the sociologist Georg Simmel—is social distance.[17]

One outcome of the management of social distance is one of several leadership paradoxes: although leaders show who they are, they are *not* easily stereotyped. Because they both show emotions and withhold them, get close and stay apart, are like us but different, their colleagues often see them as possessing enigmatic qualities.[18] They are authentic chameleons, a notion we explore in more detail in chapter 6.

Pulling all of this off demands skillful communication. Effective leaders pay careful attention to how they are seen and heard. They do not take others' perceptions for granted or assume that they are perceived similarly in every context. In chapter 7, we explore the ways in which leaders construct compelling narratives about themselves and their contexts. We also show the ways in which they identify communication channels that work for them.

Some leaders, for example, are best able to display their qualities through the platform speech; others are more effective in more intimate face-to-face settings. Part of being an effective leader is knowing which media work for you—and finding ways to exploit those. And finally, we look at their understanding of the pace and rhythm of their organization—and its implication for leadership communication.

In chapter 8, we examine the other side of the leadership equation: *followership.* If leadership is a relationship, as we believe it is, then followers also have a vital part to play. In the course of our research, we asked many followers what they wanted from their leaders. Their replies included many different things. But we also found recurring patterns. Their responses can be described under four broad headings. The four elements followers want from leaders are authenticity, significance, excitement, and community. Effective leaders understand and deliver on these four key issues.

Finally, in chapter 9, we bring these practical strands together by examining what happens when things go wrong—as they inevitably will at some point—and the ethical demands that are placed on leaders.

Inspirational Tension

You will see that there are tensions underlying each of the parts of our book: between revealing strengths but showing weaknesses, being an individual but conforming, establishing intimacy but keeping your distance. Managing these tensions lies at the heart of successful leadership. Our experience suggests excellence in one or two of these areas is insufficient for truly inspirational leadership. It is the interplay between them, guided by situation sensing, that enables great leaders to find the right style for the right moment.

You may have reached an early conclusion as you contemplate these tensions: leadership is complicated, demanding, and full of personal risk. All of this is true. Clearly, not everyone can be a leader. Many executives do not have what it takes to develop the *skillful* authenticity necessary for effective leadership. They are unable to balance the tensions at the heart of successful leadership. First, to demonstrate the maturity required to understand and deploy weakness as well as strength. Second, to know when to get close and when to remain apart from followers. Third, to appreciate that individual expression must be balanced with the need to conform *enough*.

It is not difficult, in our experience, to think of individuals who seem oblivious to their limitations yet who regularly overestimate their strengths. Senior executives, in particular, are known to systematically exaggerate their credibility with others. Equally, it is easy to think of individuals who seem stuck in the default mode of "closeness" with others and are never able to separate enough to provide objective distance. For them, being "one of the boys" fatally undermines their leadership capacity. For others, it is the reverse: their separation from others—their failure to connect—leaves them forever isolated and without the relationships necessary to sustain effective leadership.

Finally, we have been witness to countless uncomfortable examples of executives who feel that the art of leadership is to give unfettered expression to their "true selves" in bold take-it-or-leave-it fashion. They typically find that others choose to leave it. Leadership is not achieved by riding into town—cowboy fashion—and shooting it up. Skillful leaders, to continue the analogy, need to get a sense of the town, and to conform enough so that they are seen to be acting in the best interests of the townspeople, so they can lead change without being shot early on in the proceedings!

Do You Want It? Leadership and Life

All these qualities, however, are necessary but not sufficient conditions for leadership. Individuals must also *want* to be leaders—and many very talented individuals are not interested in shouldering that responsibility.[19] Others prefer to devote more time to their private lives than to their work. After all, there is more to life than work, and more to work than being the leader.

This sense of other priorities is often missed in popular discussions of leadership—particularly in business. To assume that everyone has the sheer energy, drive, and willpower required to offer inspirational leadership to others is facile. While, as we argue, each individual has unique differences that potentially can be exploited in a leadership role, each of us has to address the harsh question, Do we want it? And if we do, do we want it enough to put in the work required and make the necessary sacrifices?

It may well be that a variety of factors—unimaginative educational systems, limiting jobs, bureaucratic hierarchies—relentlessly crush the individual spirit that lies at the root of authentic leadership. Remove these barriers, and we, like others, are sure that more leaders may emerge. But it is too big a jump to assume we may all want it.

Nor is it sensible to assume that good leadership always delivers the best business results. We noted earlier that leadership is not just about results. Yet this is a trap that many modern leadership researchers have fallen into. We have become overly concerned with the ends—sometimes at the cost of neglecting the means. Interestingly, the classical understanding of leadership is primarily concerned with providing meaning. The obsession with results is a contemporary conceit and one that is partly responsible for eroding the moral dimension of leadership.

While some well-led businesses do not produce short-term results, some businesses with successful results are not well led. Enron, for example, appeared to be performing exceptionally for some years. If results were always a matter of good leadership, picking leaders would be easy. In every case the best strategy would be to go after people in companies with the best business results. But clearly, as recent painful corporate collapses and governance scandals demonstrate, things are not that easy.

Clearly, the ability to connect with followers—to inspire, excite, and arouse—is a central leadership attribute, and it is at the heart of our concerns in this book. And as we have said, *outstanding performance* is unlikely without it. But the *direction* in which leaders channel energies will vary.

The "excitement" generated in a company culture like Enron's can produce inappropriate actions and disastrous outcomes. Equally, highly motivated, well-led workforces can still fail if the market for their product collapses, or a change in government funding takes the ground from under their feet. Meanwhile, quasi-monopolistic businesses in protected markets may be performing satisfactorily with competent management and little leadership.

Yet despite all these provisos, the truth remains: great leaders can, and must, make a difference—and your capability to act as a leader can be improved. In the process, you might even make the world a better place. As we constantly urge those we work with, "Be yourself—more—with skill." In what follows we aim to show you the tough challenges involved in following this advice—and how to address them.

The led—the followers—are constantly asking the question at the heart of this book: Why should *anyone* be led by you? Why should *we* be led by you? Effective leaders must answer these questions every day in all they say and do.

TWO

Know and Show Yourself—Enough

LEADERSHIP BEGINS WITH YOU—and you will not succeed as a leader unless you have some sense of who you are. Your colleagues—potential followers—have a simple but basic need: they want to be led by a person, not by a corporate apparatchik. It is unlikely that you will be able to inspire, arouse, excite, or motivate people unless you can show them who you are, what you stand for, and what you can and cannot do.[1]

Consider Sir Martin Sorrell, the leader of the world's largest communications services company, WPP, which owns, among many companies, the JWT ad agency. Sorrell runs an organization full of creative talent. Creative people are notoriously difficult to lead or even manage but are critical to WPP's success. Indeed, WPP's mission and strategy statement begins, "To develop and manage talent; to apply that talent throughout the world."

Sorrell is a bundle of energy. He is opinionated, forthright, and clever. Over a twenty-year period, he has applied these talents to build a formidable global business. And over the years, he has learned to use some of his personal differences as a leader. Ask his colleagues about Sorrell, and a fairly consistent picture emerges.

First they will tell you of his legendarily rapid response to e-mails—whenever, wherever. It's not unusual, for example, for Sorrell to spend a working week in the United States but remain on U.K. time for those he works with in London. All of Sorrell's fifteen thousand colleagues have access to him. His message is clear: I am available. You are important. As he told us, "If someone contacts you, there's a reason. It's got nothing to do with the hierarchy. It doesn't matter if they're not a big person. There's nothing more frustrating than a voice mail and then nothing back. We're in a service business."

But this is not the only difference that he communicates. "I am seen as the boring, workaholic accountant and as a micro-manager," he told us. "But I take it as a compliment rather than an insult. Involvement is important. You've got to know what's going on." Anyone receiving a visit from Sorrell can expect some tough, one-to-one questioning—on the numbers as well as the creative side of the business. Sorrell's difference reminds people that, central though creativity is, WPP is a creative *business*.

When we talked to Sorrell's colleagues, the other thing they noted is his permanent state of dissatisfaction. He is justifiably proud of WPP's success, but constantly reminds people that "there's an awful long way to go."

Sorrell is not the most introspective character in the world—he is far too busy for that. But he knows enough about what works for him in a particular context. He uses his leadership differences—accessibility, close involvement in business detail, restlessness—to balance the creative side. These leadership assets are a foil for, on the one hand, the hierarchy and complacency that can strangle large, successful businesses and, on the other, unrestrained generation of new ideas that can lead creative organizations to lose business focus.

Private Dancers

Of course, knowing and expressing your real self is easier said than done. Workplaces often make it difficult for individuals to easily express themselves, without fear of ridicule or failure. The result? Individuals spend much of their waking hours in organizations that inhibit their authentic selves. They save their "real" selves—and much of the energy that goes with them—for their families, friends, private lives, and local communities.[2]

Although it is rarely discussed in these terms, this inability to be ourselves at work is an important element in the work/life balance debate. Our workplace cultures make it very difficult to reconcile our working selves with our private selves. Work/life balance means much more than spending time at home—it means transforming workplaces into arenas for the display of authenticity. And even in organizations where self-expression is encouraged, individuals may not be equipped to respond. Their experiences may have already damaged their capacity to both know and show themselves.[3]

The fact is that showing people who you are requires a degree of self-knowledge (or at least self-awareness) *as well as* self-disclosure. One without the other is hopeless.

We have observed individuals who know themselves well but fail to communicate this to others. Since their colleagues are not mind readers, these individuals often remain frustratingly enigmatic unless, through choice and skill, they can overcome their predilection to nondisclosure. Some introverted executives fall into this trap. The problem is made worse by the speed with which leaders are required to make an impact. Organizational time moves faster and faster. We observed a highly talented Silicon Valley executive who spoke to us of her compelling vision for the capacity of technology to transform human lives for the better. She seemed to burn with passion at the prospect. But when we asked her followers what they thought she stood for, they just didn't know. She had not found an appropriate vehicle for self-disclosure.

Equally, there are others whose efforts at self-disclosure are fatally undermined by their lack of self-knowledge. They communicate—but the image of themselves they project appears false. Colleagues typically perceive them as phony or inauthentic. You can't fake sincerity. In one case, we advised a Boston venture capitalist to spend more time with his team, who saw him as distant and aloof. He decided to take them for drinks after work on Fridays, where he exuded false bonhomie. He thought it was working well, but his followers saw him as a fake.

So to *be* yourself, you must *know* yourself and *show* yourself—enough. (Put another way, you must be sufficiently self-aware and also prepared to self-declare.)

Just as self-knowledge is never complete; neither is self-disclosure. Effective leaders know *enough* and show *enough* to maximize their leadership impact.

A great deal of academic attention has been focused on personal identity. We are not about to revisit and rework these theories. We are neither equipped to do so nor do we see it as central to understanding effective leadership. There is already a rich and extensive psychological literature that addresses, for example, the related concepts of "self," "identity," and "personality."[4]

Even if you do not know the research, you are probably familiar with one of its spin-offs: the extensive range of popular diagnostic instruments and psychometric tools that can help you to understand "who you are": your particular strengths, weaknesses, aptitudes, personality attributes, and so on.

Self-assessment instruments are often helpful. They can help us understand, for example, the kinds of activities, jobs, or careers we might find most fulfilling. But taken to extremes, they can also be limiting. How we as individuals—and our identities—develop is rarely as "planned" as those who promote the assessments suggest. Discovering who we are is likely to be a lifetime process involving continual testing and learning, trial and error, and many twists and turns along the way. Every twist results in learning, and learning is always done in conjunction with others.

These primarily psychological approaches to personal identity have their limits if we are trying to understand leadership. Leadership is a relationship. Inevitably, you show what you know about yourself *in context, to others.* This opens the possibility that you will show different aspects of who you are at different times and in different places—and that the creation of self is also a lifelong process.

What Works for You?

Given this lifelong journey of exploration, it is clearly unreasonable to expect that skillful self-disclosure should rest upon complete self-knowledge. Effective leaders rarely have perfect self-insight. Some are too fixed on their overarching purpose to worry much about themselves, while others display narcissistic properties that badly distort their sense of self.[5] They are only human.

What characterizes effective leaders is a sense of *what works for them with others*. As we noted earlier, this does not necessarily require that they have a deep understanding of how and why it works. What we observe in effective leaders is primarily a matter of self-awareness. As they interact with others, leaders seem better able to learn how they are seen and how they can actively shape others' perceptions in the formation of their identity.

Think back to an experience that is certainly not unique to those who go on to become great leaders. Most of us can probably recall from our early teenage dating years a time when, excessively concerned with dress and appearance, we had favorite items of clothing. Remember the lucky shirt, the winning shoes, the special perfume, that seemed to work for us? You may even recall your anger when the special shirt had not been ironed or the favorite perfume ran out.

Your investigations may have gone further. You may have sought to test, for example, where your differences had their greatest impact: on the dance floor, in the coffee bar, or walking in the park? In fact, your adolescence probably marks the first time that you consciously thought through and tried out how to make the most of your differences in a way that might excite others.

Effective leaders keep working at this art. They develop a close understanding of their differences. In particular, they become aware of what is different about them that makes them attractive to others. They learn to use these differences to their advantage in a leadership role.

Consider Bill Gates. What is different about Gates is that he is the ultimate computer geek. He has taken a pejorative stereotype and turned it to his advantage. When it comes to the computer industry, Gates knows what he is talking about. He knows the technology inside out. Gates's consistent display of his "geekiness" tells us something very important about him and his company. Over time it has become an increasingly skillful use of self-image.

Think back to Sir Richard Branson, skillfully using his physical appearance to communicate personal identity in an attractive way. One way in which former President Clinton communicates his personal appeal is through a handshake held for a fraction of a second longer than expected. Those who experience this invariably notice and comment on it.

In the United Kingdom in the 1980s, John Harvey Jones—the boss of the country's largest manufacturing company, ICI—was famous in the business world for his long hair and loud kipper ties. Did this uniquely explain his success? Of course not. But it demonstrated his clever ability to develop differences that communicated that he was adventurous, entrepreneurial, and unique—he was John Harvey Jones. Was it a deliberate strategy? To begin with, we doubt it—more a matter of personal taste and preference. But over time, we suspect Harvey Jones began to realize that these were differences that worked for him. They helped him stand out from the crowd—and they sent the right messages.

Even in societies that, through Western eyes, appear to stress homogeneity and conformity, there are opportunities for leaders to skillfully express their difference. For example, take the legendary figure of Akio Morita, the founder of Sony. He was widely known for his boundless energy. At 72 he was still playing tennis at 7:00 A.M.—often with much younger people. He challenged entrenched beliefs in Japanese society. In his book *Never Mind School Records,* for instance, he argued that school achievements are not important in judging the ability to do business.[6] He completely rethought the nature of U.S.-Japan economic relations, and Sony became the first Japanese company to be listed on the New York Stock Exchange. More than that, he was perhaps the first significant business leader to understand the idea of an organization that served customers, shareholders, and employees on a global basis irrespective of the company's nation of origin.

But remember, leadership is nonhierarchical. We have observed people using their differences in order to build their leadership capability at all levels of the organization. Consider Carol Browne, a nurse we encountered in a New York hospital. She is interpersonally highly skilled. Indeed, you could describe her as charming. What is really remarkable is that she uses her charm to weld together a team of nurses, administrators, doctors, and paramedics built around care for patients. Carol's charm is real and used for an overarching purpose.

To begin with, this is unconscious. But at some point, individuals make conscious choices about what works for them and how much they are prepared to adapt.

Consider the case of Paulette. She runs a sales force for Procter & Gamble. At first meeting, she seems a shy, rather retiring kind of person. Indeed, our first observation was that there was nothing exceptional about her. And then we observed her with her team. Two powerful leadership differences were on display to great effect. First, the sheer analytical power of her intellect: every aspect of the market, the competition, and the products had been analyzed, to the delight of her followers. Second, her passion for winning excited everyone around her to higher performance. Rarely have we seen a leader in whom this obsession was so effectively translated into a leadership asset.

Broadcasting Leadership

One of the leaders we have spent the most time with is Greg Dyke, the former director general of the British Broadcasting Corporation (BBC), the United Kingdom's publicly funded broadcaster. Along with the National Health Service, the BBC is often seen as the jewel in the crown of modern Britain, an achievement the nation can be proud of.

Indeed, the BBC probably attracts more press coverage than any other organization in the United Kingdom. Running a national institution is a big, difficult job. The BBC employs approximately twenty-five thousand people and has an annual income of around £3 billion. With all this money and attention comes a certain amount of criticism. As Greg Dyke observed, if your programs get more viewers, you are accused of "dumbing down," and if they do not, then you are accused of "wasting taxpayers' money."

Dyke's tenure at the BBC was characterized by significant change. He increased expenditure on programs and cut costs on administrative support (symbolically reducing the BBC's fleet of chauffeur-driven cars). But most impressively, he transformed the morale of the staff, encouraging them to put "creativity and innovation at the heart of everything we do."

Physically, Greg Dyke does not look like a typical BBC boss. He is compact in build, with a distinctly receding hairline. (In fact, it has retreated rather a long way.) He dresses sharply and in a slightly showbiz style. All his suits come from the same tailor and definitely don't look "old school." He walks quickly and purposefully. His whole demeanor radiates energy—he was once a promising 400 meters runner. Even in his early fifties, he communicates a restless vibrancy, like a boxer before a fight.

He tends to make direct eye contact (except when delivering bad news). He talks with a definite London accent, not a Cockney accent; he is actually from West London, but his voice is certainly characterized by the urban rhythms of a born Londoner. He has a cheery, hail-fellow-well-met demeanor, and his passions include science education, museums, and, perhaps above all, soccer, especially Manchester United (of which he was formerly a director).

In other words, he is not at all as you would expect a director general of the BBC to be. Greg Dyke is definitely not of the Establishment. He is clearly different. And yet, Greg Dyke utilized these aspects of his real self, in context and skillfully, to communicate a different vision for the BBC from that of his predecessors. He set about creating an organization that was highly stimulating and a fun place to work, where making and broadcasting programs that enrich peoples' lives was rediscovered as the core purpose. His failure—he was forced to resign in 2004 after a high-profile political face-off with the British government—cannot be attributed to an absence of leadership. (The reasons for his departure are explored later.)

Observing Dyke carefully, you realize that his presentation of self is both knowing and skillful. He knows and shows adroitly. He has learned, over time, when to use his clear differences to greatest effect. There is even a degree of playfulness in the aspects of himself that he reveals to those he aspires to lead. His energy and personality are communicated to his followers.

On the evening he left the BBC, staff gave him an unprecedented and emotional departure. A large crowd of employees gathered in the BBC building to applaud. Many were in tears. Dyke was a leader they believed in and were prepared to follow. The reasons for the emotional outpouring, as we shall see, lie with Dyke's authentic leadership style.

Different Strokes

You don't have to be a corporate superman to be a great leader. The late Darwin E. Smith, for example, was the CEO of the paper company Kimberly-Clark for twenty years. He was described as shy, unpretentious, and even awkward. With his heavy black-rimmed glasses and unfashionable suits, Smith looked more like a small-town hick than a corporate titan—an image he used to his advantage, both to stay close to the business and to deflect unwanted outside attention. Smith was a geek before geeks became fashionable. Yet, under his quiet rule, Kimberly-Clark outperformed not just competitors like Procter & Gamble, but also GE, Hewlett-Packard, Coca-Cola, 3M, and every other star of corporate America.[7]

Many more leaders maximize the impact of their difference. Think of the current mayor of London, Ken Livingstone. He dresses like a slightly careworn school teacher, speaks in a distinctive nasal way, and has a passion for newts. He makes a point of regularly commuting to work on the public subway system. On at least two occasions, he has used his leadership to change London's transport system—by dramatically reducing fares and, more recently, by introducing congestion charging for central London road traffic. Few other politicians could have introduced such a potentially unpopular idea without losing office. Livingstone was returned to office in 2004 with a comfortable majority. He succeeds because people believe that he really identifies with Londoners. They may disagree with his political beliefs, but are still prepared to vote for him because he radiates concern about London.

Sometimes the personal differences perceived by colleagues as important are not quite what you might expect. Take Franz Humer, the chairman of health-care company Roche. In our work with hundreds of his colleagues over recent years, we have often asked them about the differences he communicates. They list many characteristics, among them his entrepreneurial flair, marketing insight, and passion for innovation. But what do they put at the top of the list? His communication of emotion—particularly through the use of his piercing blue eyes. This observation is all the more surprising coming from rational Swiss scientists.

Our first meeting with Humer was revealing. One of the authors was ushered into his large office overlooking the Rhine and shown to a table in a far corner of the room. A polite opening question was addressed to Dr. Humer. He rose silently from his desk and strode to the window to gaze for several moments at the Rhine. Then he returned to his desk and lit a large cigar. He walked slowly to the corner where we sat, drew upon the cigar, peered carefully over his lowered half-glasses, and finally answered the question.

From question to answer was probably around a minute, but it felt as if two hundred years had passed. At first sight, this might appear to be yet another CEO using the trappings of office as an excuse for arrogant behavior. But this would be a misinterpretation. As his colleagues later confirmed, Humer is a master of using silence and facial expression to communicate his emotional intensity and thoughtfulness. These are appropriate leadership values if you are running a complex, knowledge-based business.

Franz Humer also believes that personal passion is what drives innovation. Watch him make a public presentation, and you witness a carefully honed performance. His personal emotions are skillfully revealed to engage and energize others.[8]

"At a senior executive meeting, we ended the day by enjoying a wonderful concert," one of his colleagues told us. "The violinist was a beautiful woman, and the performance was excellent. At the close, the audience warmly applauded. Sensing a greater acknowledgment was in order, Humer rose from his seat, walked over and scooped up the contents of a vase of flowers adorning the baby grand, and presented them to the violinist. His panache, creativity, and impulsiveness were captured beautifully in an instant. The act brought yet another round of applause and genuine laughter. This memory for me is the best of Franz—impulse, act, and outcome all beautifully aligned."

Reality Testing

There is an almost endless list of differences that individuals might communicate. But any attempt to create the definitive list of leadership attributes is futile. This is because the differences must be authentic to you as a leader. They must be significant, real, and perceived.

Think back to Martin Sorrell. Does he show his personal differences knowingly? Yes. Are they significant in the context of WPP? Undoubtedly. Are they real? Utterly.

Clearly, all of the leaders we have cited so far are using difference to signify something about who they are and what they stand for: Branson's challenging nonconformity, Clinton's interpersonal charm, Harvey Jones's entrepreneurial pizzazz, Bill Gates's technological "geekiness," Carol Browne's care for patients, Greg Dyke's man-of-the-people approachability, Darwin E. Smith's modesty, Ken Livingstone's identification with Londoners, and Franz Humer's emotional intensity.

In all these examples, leaders are using personal differences that work for them appropriately in context. They convey the right message—and they are real. Ultimately, it is this sense of authentic self-expression that makes them so convincing.

But how do we know they are real? This is a difficult question to answer. There are large and complex philosophical issues here. Ultimately, we are helped by the tremendous human capacity to instinctively recognize behavior that is not authentic. And when followers spot this, it is very hard for leaders to recover.

This, of course, is the problem with many of the leadership recipe books written by successful executives. Even if it is un-intended by the authors, there is a significant risk that readers conclude that by mimicking what worked for others, they too can become great leaders. Nothing could be further from the truth. Only one person does Jack Welch convincingly—and that's Jack Welch. Ditto Lee Iacocca, Bill Gates, Steve Jobs, Richard Branson, and all the other "legendary" figures held up before us as leader-ship role models through the years. The challenge for all aspiring leaders is to become more knowing and more skilled at disclosing themselves, rather than trying to become someone else.

This means digging deep, using what you have, and keeping a continual reality check with others about how you are perceived. Digging deep often means going back to your origins, a theme we will explore in some detail later in the chapter. It's no surprise, for example, to learn that Martin Sorrell explains his view that people all over the organization should be listened to by reference to his father's strong ideals. He believed, Martin told us, "that every one has value." Similarly, Greg Dyke feels he inherits his "man of the people" style from his father, who would "talk to everyone, includ-ing the road sweeper, and would laugh at people who took them-selves too seriously."

Authentic leaders are not imitations. To remain real in their relationships with followers, they also take constant reality checks. As Roche Pharmaceuticals CEO Bill Burns told us, "You have to keep your feet on the ground when others want to put you on a pedestal. After a while on a pedestal, you stop hearing the truth. It's filtered by the henchmen, and they read you so well, they know what you want to hear. You end up as the queen bee in the hive, with no relationship with the worker bees. My wife and secretary are fully empowered if they ever see me getting a bit uppity to give me a thumping great hit over the head!"

But of course, this is not the only way in which Bill seeks feedback. For several years now, we have worked with him and his top team using extensive 360-degree interview and questionnaire appraisals of individual leadership style. As with all the most effective leaders, there is a continual attempt by Bill to open all channels, formal and informal, to learn about how others see him. This is not a Machiavellian maneuver, but a simple desire to learn more about himself and how he comes across to others.

On the Leadership Stage

Bill Burns's wise practices remind us of the care that effective leaders demonstrate in checking how they are perceived by others— and which differences are attributed to them.

There is inevitably a theatrical element to leadership: it is a performance for the benefit of followers. Playing to your differences—and finding ways to effectively display them—is, in varying degrees, a conscious performance with an end in mind. But this does not make it insincere. Good leaders want to do well for themselves and their followers, and they will invest themselves in their roles. But as these examples show, they will always reserve enough space to see themselves in the role, to assess their performance and how well it fits the needs of others and the context.

Sometimes the surprise element of communication can be devastating. We met a social worker in Brazil who decided to enter the world of the local gangs by starting and coaching a soccer team. The gangs initially viewed this gentle philanthropist with great suspicion. What worked for him was that he was one of the hardest tacklers around. He showed even the hardest that he was tough; and despite the emphasis on silky skills in Brazilian football, there is nothing more admired than a strong tackle. He won first respect and later love.

Consider Jean Tomlin. At the time we interviewed her, she was HR director at the retailer Marks & Spencer.[9] Jean is a black woman in one of the most senior HR positions in the United Kingdom. She reflects, with much insight, on the appropriate presentation of self:

> Before I go into a situation, I try to understand what it is they will be thinking. I prepare what I am going to say and who I am going to be in that context. Going to a function or into a room full of people I don't know, I try and do a bit of homework to understand what I am going into. I want to be me, but I am channeling parts of me to context. What you get is a segment of me. It is not fabricated or a façade—it's the bits that are relevant for that situation.
>
> I have a particular way of being when engaging as a leader. I have been told my eyes become more focused, I speak more slowly—it's clear we have a task to discuss. I take on another aspect—clear, focused, seriousness of face—but it's just part of the spectrum, and people that know me understand that.

In our conversations with John Latham, the head teacher of an award-winning school, we encountered a similar thoughtfulness about when and how to display differences. Despite all his natural enthusiasm, vision, and passion, Latham started in his new role as head of the publicly funded school in a deliberately low-key fashion. His predecessor had pushed for fast change over a four-year period. This left many staff concerned about yet another "shake-up" on Latham's arrival.

"I spent a long time thinking about my first sentence as head teacher," Latham told us. "My predecessor had used his surname and was seen to be in a hurry. 'My name is John,' I began. I explained that teaching and learning were my drives—and that I found them difficult. I listened to what excited them and what held them back—and I went to their classrooms to listen. Lots of them said we want the door handle fixed, or the clocks aren't working. And that's where I started, with the small things. I fixed some of that the first afternoon, before I went home. It quickly removed some of the barriers. I wanted to get a reputation for getting things done."

John Latham illustrates the care effective leaders take to communicate the "right" differences as fast as possible—in his case, a huge personal passion for education and development, but combined with humility, preparedness to listen, and a willingness to personally address the mundane details that affect day-to-day performance.

Impressions formed early are often hard to shift. When Simon Gulliford became marketing director of Barclays Bank, he found it difficult to fit his Welsh charm and directness into the company's somewhat political culture. Simon is an ex–rugby player from the industrial valleys of South Wales. He still speaks with a marked Welsh accent, not the fashionable, polished kind either, but closer to the tones of his firebrand grandfather. He planned a series of road shows to take his ideas out to the branches, and we urged him to advance his schedule for them because we knew he would be effective. He is one of the most electric presenters we know, a speaker whose timing, personality, and wit are guaranteed to win over any audience. And sure enough, after the road shows, staff were eating out of his hand. Gulliford used the presentations as a way of demonstrating his vision and his extraordinarily engaging and persuasive communication skills.

Well Cast

Peter Brabeck, the CEO of Nestlé, is pictured on the cover of a Nestlé environmental report sitting in the Swiss mountains wearing climbing clothes. In another publication, the Nestlé *Leadership and Management Principles*, he is dressed in a dark suit outside the corporate headquarters. As he told us, "I wanted to use the image of the mountaineer because water and the environment are emotional issues. But the photo is not artificial. That's what I wear at weekends. I'm a climber. It has to be authentic. You can't try to be something else. In the mountaineering picture it's a human being talking. In the suit in front of our offices I am talking for the institution. Both photographs work well. But they are different. And neither is artificial."

As the identification and transmission of personal differences is refined, it is likely that both the leader and the followers implicitly acknowledge that a role is being played. But skillful players will show enough of their real personal differences to demonstrate their authenticity. They will also create situations that enable them to demonstrate their differences.

When he was senior vice president for operations at Lufthansa, Thomas Sattelberger said, "I had to create my own stages," to get the airline's message across to its twenty-five thousand employees. Sattelberger is a very talented public speaker, who seems to maintain eye contact with everyone in the room. He says he is most effective not face-to-face but "face to many faces." So he chose a format of town meetings, at which he could address up to two hundred employees at a time. "People look at my eyes," he says. "So I usually take a chair and put it in the middle of the stage. I don't want the table and the overhead projector. People react to my face." He's right, and his performance makes him an effective leader.

Of course, such role playing has to be handled with care. The danger is that leaders are thought to be showing off their superior strengths. This normally produces failure rather than success. This is what seemed to happen during Robert Horton's tenure as chairman and CEO of BP during the early 1990s. Horton's conspicuous display of his considerable—indeed, daunting—intelligence sometimes led others to see him as arrogant and self-aggrandizing. His confident approach had worked well for him during his stint in the United States, but it was less well received back at corporate offices in the United Kingdom. Indeed, these personal differences eventually contributed to Horton's dismissal just three years after he was appointed to the position.

Similarly, there is a story that the former England national soccer coach, Glenn Hoddle, once asked his star player, David Beckham, to practice a particular maneuver. When Beckham couldn't do it, Hoddle—once a brilliant player himself—said, "Here, I'll show you how." He performed the maneuver flawlessly, but in that moment he lost the team. The other players saw it as a public humiliation of Beckham. Hoddle was subsequently named "chocolate" by his players because they believed that he thought of himself as "good enough to eat."

This is the familiar trap of the narcissistic leader, a well-worked theme in the leadership literature.[10] What our colleague Jay Conger calls the "shadow side of charisma" leads individuals to become self-serving and to have an exaggerated sense of their own abilities and self-importance.[11] In our terms these leaders are aware of their differences but distort them, eventually blowing them out of all proportion, often with disastrous consequences. The list of examples is long: from Edwin Land with Polaroid in the 1970s to Steve Jobs at Apple, Jan Carlzon at SAS, and Pehr Gyllenhammer at Volvo.[12] All developed a sense of infallibility that put their companies at risk.

There Is a Leader in the Team

Effective leaders deploy their differences to serve both their own *and* the team's interests. In effect, they convey the reassuring message that "if you fall, I will catch you." Their people know the leader has the strengths to carry out the task but that he will also step aside and let them develop their own strengths. In effect, this is what typically protects such leaders from the charge of "showing off."

The yachtsman and adventurer Pete Goss is a powerful example. He is perhaps best known for his heroic rescue—in the teeth of a hurricane—of a French competitor in the Vendee Globe single-handed round-the-world yacht race. For this, Pete was awarded the Legion d'Honneur, France's highest award for gallantry. He has also been awarded an MBE (Member of the British Empire) and been named Yachtsman of the Year. Pete has a string of other achievements to his name, including the development of a revolutionary catamaran sponsored by Team Philips.

There is no doubt that Pete is a big character, driven by a fierce personal passion and a determination to succeed. Once he has set his heart on something, he will move heaven and earth to make it happen. Read his résumé, and you will see he has plenty to boast about. But he is not the larger-than-life figure that you might expect. Meet him face-to-face, and you will encounter a modest, self-effacing, and (by his own admission) shy man. He will tell you how he was terrified of standing in front of a crowd of strangers to make a speech and how much he has learned from other people; the novices he has trained on boats, the corporate representatives who helped him with fund-raising, the journalists who interviewed him. He will tell you in a matter-of-fact way that the point is to get on with things and enjoy it. "It's not a question of is the glass half full or half empty. What we say is drink the bastard anyway!" And above all, he will remind you that a "single-handed" yacht race is a misnomer, that all his achievements have been built upon the efforts of a "very large family" whose complementary strengths are what eventually produce success.

It has become popular over recent years to brand the style exemplified by Goss as "quiet leadership."[13] There is no doubt that Pete is able to impose himself and communicate his leadership assets in a low-key, understated way. But more than this, we would argue, he personally exemplifies what he encourages in all those around him. His differences are significant. He is living proof that modest individuals can achieve great things if they set their hearts upon it, that we all "have a giant within," to use one of Pete's favorite quotations.

Listening to Learn

Our overwhelming impression is that in developing their self-awareness, effective leaders pursue a clear and simple strategy: they try things out and get feedback. Many years ago the psychologist David Kolb mapped out the preferences that individuals have for particular ways of learning. He describes learning through concrete experience, reflection and observation, active experimentation, and, finally, abstract conceptualization.[14]

Our observations are that effective leaders rely heavily on experience and experimentation. They do engage in reflection but rarely arrive at their leadership capability through theory. It is ironic, then, that classic business school classroom experience is geared mostly around abstract conceptualizing with a little reflection and observation.

Peter Brabeck of Nestlé observes, "I have difficulty in explaining leadership in an entirely rational or analytical way. There's a part of it that you cannot explain. Yes, you can improve techniques, of course—I am not against it. But leadership has to be based on experience and situations. When I was a young lad, I had to do military experience. Think of it. I was seventeen years old. It was a very interesting experience. Basically, for the first time in your life, you are being treated like dirt! And it's interesting how you react. We had some trying to commit suicide. They couldn't take it. How you digest those experiences is important, and it teaches you a lot about yourself."

Other leaders seem to be able to build wider experiences into their daily working lives and careers. David Gardner, former European CEO of Electronic Arts Inc. (EA), the electronic games developer, is a long way from his California roots, yet he relished the differences he encountered across the various EA territories for which he was responsible. In our discussions he regularly talked with enthusiasm about the challenge of translating and applying the EA culture in the contrasting contexts of the United Kingdom, France, and Germany. In his work schedule, he made a point of regular visits to each of the EA European offices, listening to as many people as he could—all over and beyond the organization: the sales force, office staff, engineers, and customers. He deliberately avoided being captured by the local senior executives. At the point we interviewed him, he was about to take a sabbatical—time for some more new experiences—with plans including time in Japan and some business school teaching.

Of course, trying things out—active experimentation as the learning theorists call it—often means operating outside your comfort zone. Head teacher John Latham describes the atmosphere at his school as "a little on the edge," "a bit risky," "not entirely comfortable"—and much of this comes from his own drive to keep trying new things. Not all his initiatives are greeted with universal enthusiasm. When he suggested children set their own tests, they thought he was "off the planet." One of his teaching colleagues described his empowerment philosophy as "claptrap." None of this dampened John's missionary zeal—it simply taught him to make adjustments in his style, pace, and approach as he has sought to deploy his unique differences.

Similarly, David Gardner's major concern when he came to Europe was that his staff might mistake his genuine concern for people, his desire to foster involvement and celebrate teamwork, as cynical, American corporate brainwashing. He deliberately set out to adapt his style to allow more questioning and debate of his own and the wider EA values.

When David announced he was about to take a year's sabbatical, one of his creative staff accused him of "forgetting" about his colleagues—proof he was no more than a representative of the company machine. David began a dialog with him, explaining his apprehension and uncertainty about his year off. His colleague was stunned by his honesty—and quickly forgot the stereotype of the corporate man.

In each of these cases, there is evidence of leaders learning to use their differences—David Gardner's concern for people, John Latham's passion for empowerment—such that they work for them as positive attributes in different contexts.

Socially Authentic

Authentic leaders are prepared to go beyond their comfort zones. But what is also notable is that most successful leaders we have observed and interviewed seem to be very "grounded" individuals. They have a very clear sense of who they are and where they come from. They are comfortable with their origins.

Greg Dyke, for example, is forever retelling stories of how his father would talk to everyone as an equal. He tells the stories with intense pride, as if they explained who he has become. Simon Gulliford at Barclays often talks of his grandfather. He amusingly tells how his grandfather retains the view that he is utterly irresistible to women even though he is well into his seventies. Gulliford explains his own powerful sense of self-confidence as deriving from his grandfather's faith in him.

Our observations have led us to the view that an authentic sense of self arises from individuals coming to terms with their own biography—and a critical part of this is to understand how their origins have come to shape them. Origins, of course, can be conceived of in many ways. For some, family origin is most salient; for others, it may be class, gender, ethnicity, social status, religion, or geographical locale.

The ways in which individuals conceive of their origins may vary between cultures. For example, in the United States, locale may act as a particularly powerful source of identity, while in many European countries, class and status remain highly salient, often in mysterious ways. In many parts of Asia, family remains the most significant way of conceptualizing origins.[15]

Despite these aggregate cultural differences, our evidence suggests that leaders conceive of their origins through multiple lenses, where all of the variables operate in a kind of palimpsest: one factor layered on top of another. Thus each individual may be the subject of multiple determinations.

Rick Dobbis (of whom you will hear more later) had a highly successful career with Sony Music. He is a Jewish, Brooklyn, New Yorker, and he never forgets that he is all those things. He is not an Orthodox Jew, but the central ritual of Yom Kippur is honored in a traditional yet somehow intensely contemporary way: "It's a good thing to think about all the things you could've done differently— made peoples' lives a little better. It's a religious tradition in a thoroughly modern context." His desk is a shrine to the original Brooklyn Dodgers (Dodger is also the name of his dog). He showed us a photograph of his grandparents' bakery in Brooklyn.

His sense of origins goes even deeper. In a discussion about new patterns of migration from eastern Europe into the United Kingdom, he pointedly reminded us of his own eastern European origins and the human reasons for migration. As C. Wright Mills memorably observed, something special takes place at the intersection between history and biography.[16]

Rob Murray, CEO of one of Australasia's biggest beer companies, Lion Nathan, is an accomplished executive and a leader of considerable power. His educational achievements took him to Cambridge University. His career has taken him all over the world. But he has never lost touch with his own British working-class roots. He still has the same direct and forthright manner of speaking. His beloved soccer team is still Walsall, a lowly team from a town in the heart of the industrial Midlands. From the other side of the world, he still makes a point of tracking their results each weekend throughout the season. Like Rick Dobbis, he is another leader who, despite his considerable success in business, is at ease with his origins.

And it's not just those at the very top who use biography to lead. In a small office in a suburban Chicago bank, sits Claire—a long-term bank employee who has made it to back-office super-visor. The walls are covered with photographs of her family—all from in or near Chicago—and her early experiences as a promising swimmer. She uses these icons of her life to explain to her staff who she is and what she stands for.

Where and Who

However, whatever the complexities of the cultural variation, we have been consistently struck by the ways in which effective leaders can articulate the relationship between where they came from and who they are. Many of the observed exemplify this point. Niall FitzGerald, former cochairman at Unilever, speaks often and with insight about his Irishness and the influence of his mother on both his moral and political worldview. Anthony Bergmans, his cochairman colleague, remains obstinately the Dutch farmer de-spite his elevated status as joint chairman. It is demonstrated in his dress, even his gait; and though Bergmans is less open about its influence than Fitzgerald is of his own origins, it is clear that, for Bergmans, his origins are a matter of some pride. They are part of who he has become.

Ian Powell, leader of the Business Recovery Services U.K. practice for the global professional services firm PricewaterhouseCoopers, is equally aware of how his social origins have made him who he is.

He hails from the United Kingdom's former industrial heartland: the Black Country. It has left him with a distinct West Midlands accent, not often heard in the boardrooms of major U.K. companies. His family came from the respectable working class, and his father eventually became a works manager, only to give it up to become a schoolteacher. It seemed a more interesting, even honorable way to use one's life, he explained. His family was Methodist, and this too has left its mark on his moral position. To observe Powell now in a leadership position is to see these complex factors rearranged in a skillful way: the disarming accent, the humility, the openness, the ease with popular culture—sport, rock music—all known to himself and disclosed to his followers.

In stark contrast, Sir Christopher Bland, chairman of BT and former chairman of the BBC, is equally unashamed of who he is: a patrician, Tory Ulsterman, who "likes to be in charge." It doesn't work for everyone, but at least he is clear about exactly where he is coming from—speech ringing with social-class markers and littered with Latin phrases expresses exactly who he is. Take it or leave it. It must be authentic, whatever it is.

Other examples are more complex. Patti Cazzato, a senior executive working with retailing giant Gap at the time we met, is from rural Kansas. In her job she has to deal with sophisticated, urban New York designers. Patti told us that when she began these working relationships, she felt slightly overawed by the encounters—as if she were still wearing Kansas dust on her clothes. She felt gauche and inhibited among her new colleagues. It took a trip back to her roots for her to rediscover herself and bring her own authenticity back into her leadership: to be herself in the new context.

Comfort with origins, then, is one aspect of people who combine self-awareness with the ability to disclose. But it is not the only one. As individuals move through life, they experience mobility—social and geographical, within and between organizations, across and up and down hierarchies. And this experience of mobility can disrupt an individual's sense of self.

In the United States, for example, high levels of social mobility have been associated by some social critics with societal symptoms of rootlessness and alienation. This was memorably captured in David Reisman's classic study, *The Lonely Crowd*.[17] In contrast, our observation of effective leaders is that as well as being comfortable with their origins, they are also at ease with mobility. They take themselves with them to new contexts. They adapt, of course, but they retain their authenticity in the new situation. (This is discussed further in chapter 5.)

Growing Your Own

If comfort with origins and ease with mobility help with authenticity, how can aspiring leaders grow these capabilities? What follows is a list of pragmatic suggestions drawn from our interview material. Not all of these will work for everyone; try to find techniques that help you. But if you cannot develop a refined awareness of what works for you, then your leadership abilities will be limited.

- **Seek out new experiences and new contexts.** This can involve changes as small as seeking to lead outside your function or as large as seeking to lead in an entirely different context. We interviewed a tough CFO who worked in a drug rehab unit on a one-month sabbatical. He reported that it forced him to reexamine his own leadership behaviors and to reconnect with his fundamental values. One critical characteristic here is that his hierarchical position as CFO meant nothing in the new context. There was just him and those he sought to lead and help.

A corollary of this is that to develop self-knowledge, you should avoid comfort zones and routines. Developing self-knowledge requires active experimentation. Routines, in and of themselves, inhibit this experimentation drive.

- **Get honest feedback.** Effective leaders seek out sources of straight feedback. We have had very good results from carefully collected workplace feedback (including 360-degree feedback). But there is also a role for coaches who can give an external perspective. But perhaps the best feedback comes from honest colleagues and those who know us best: our family and friends.

- **Explore biography.** Many of the leaders we have both interviewed and observed have had a deep and intimate knowledge of the contexts that made them what they are. Explore these; talk to others who may share the same experiences. Self-knowledge grows from coming to terms with the events that make us what we are.

- **Return to roots.** Patti Cazzato's trip back to Texas reinforced the sense of self. Simon Gulliford takes a short golfing holiday every year with a group of old friends from Pontypridd, the Welsh town where he grew up. Spend time with people who know you without the trappings of organizational power.

- **Find a third place.** The American writer Ray Oldenburg has put forward the convincing argument that after work and family, we all need a third place: somewhere we can make associations and develop a sense of self, freed from the obligations of work and family roles.[18] For the fictional characters in the U.S. comedy drama *Cheers*, the bar illustrates such a third place.

Knowing yourself, being yourself, and disclosing yourself are vital ingredients of effective leadership. In chapter 3, we show how, on the basis of this knowledge, you can start to take leadership risks.

THREE

Take Personal Risks

REMEMBER THE SCHOOL HEADMASTER, John Latham? He deliberately began his tenure in low-key, pragmatic fashion, fixing the small things that got in the way of his staff and their performance. This helped him connect to his new colleagues and win their confidence.[1]

It did not take long for Latham's personal energy and passion to shine through. The school was quickly designated as a "beacon school": a model of what can be achieved in public education.

As is virtually always the case, John Latham has flaws that represent the flip side of his strengths. His enthusiasm can overwhelm him to the point where he has trouble, for example, organizing his work and managing his time. Latham's secretary is grateful for the invention of cell phones. After she persuaded him to get one—and then to keep it switched on—she was finally able to keep some sort of track of where he was. Before that, he could be just about anywhere. His limited appreciation of his diary's schedule meant that visitors would turn up, and Latham might be out picking up litter or having an informal discussion with an off-duty teacher. But his secretary's exasperation is thoroughly affectionate. It is precisely this combination of strengths and weaknesses that makes him a *real* person—and an *authentic leader*.

Latham doesn't look the part of a charismatic leader. He is slight in build and has a large facial birthmark. But audiences forget that the instant he begins to talk. The son of a preacher, he is an exceptional public speaker, with innate talent and skills absorbed in childhood. His passion is to help everyone he can reach to achieve their full human potential. His conviction is that everyone has good qualities to be brought out; and his authenticity can convince parents instantly that his school is a place where their children will thrive.

He communicates his energy to the school's staff, and he uses the status and extra resources of a beacon school to continually improve it. He does this by luring talented teachers, for instance, or getting designated as a technology school to gain extra funds for computers. Often his staffers think he is getting carried away and aiming too high, but they say he usually comes back with the prize—or at least a net gain.

More than this, his staff are unanimous in their praise for Latham's ability to recognize their individual talents, encourage their contributions, and keep up spirits when the going gets tough. All are impressed by his handwritten personal notes, his acknowledgment of birthdays, and his sense of when to be supportive. One young teacher still learning the ropes related a story of an especially tough day at work. The next day she received a reenergizing one-line note from Latham. It simply said, "I think you are marvelous." The headmaster had noticed and responded with encouragement. His timing was impeccable.

Caring Enough to Lead

Real leaders genuinely care about their cause. Latham is passionate about every facet of his school, large and small. He often walks around with a trash bin and a nail-tipped stick, picking up litter. Some kids make fun of that activity, and you might say it's hardly the best use of a headmaster's time. But the message gets through. John Latham really cares about the school and is prepared to practice what he preaches.

In common with the other authentic leaders we have observed, Latham also cares enough to make himself vulnerable. This involves revealing his weaknesses as well as his strengths. He is prepared to let his followers see his human foibles—to admit that he is imperfect.[2]

Latham acknowledges that he must be "exhausting" to work for. He has learned to slow down (a little) on "endless" new ideas and initiatives by adopting twenty-four-hour personal "cool-off" periods before decisions are made. He also clearly signals to his most trusted staff that their role is to temper some of his enthusiasms. Colleagues are charged to pick up on the detail, to watch the numbers. Basically, they prevent his weaknesses from having a negative effect on the school. But ultimately, there's a limit to this kind of adaptation.

Is Latham still to be found out in the grounds picking up litter and chatting with the children while an "important" visitor waits?

Yes. Does he realize that some of the children make fun of him for doing this? Of course. Will he change? Unlikely. John Latham, like other good leaders, has come to a mature decision about which "weaknesses" are "him." He is aware of the foibles that can actually work to his advantage—as well as the ones he and others will simply have to live with.

Showing Your Foibles

Showing yourself as a leader always involves risks, and the risks are personal. To imagine that you can act as an effective leader without putting a little bit of yourself on the line is an illusion. And a dangerous one.

As John Latham demonstrates, showing weakness—and in his case a degree of eccentricity—is typically a by-product of the authentic leader's overarching goals and passions. Because they really care about the purpose of the organization, they reveal themselves: what it is they care about, why they care about it, and how they believe the organization can achieve its stated goals. But there is also an element of detachment that enables authentic leaders to monitor and adjust their own effectiveness. Initially, just as with the positive personal differences discussed in the last chapter, we suspect that the revelation of weakness is unknowing. But once leaders begin to recognize the impact of displays of fallibility, self-awareness increases—and with it the option to modify their behavior, if only in a small way.

Another example of a leader whose passion leads her to reveal weakness is Anita Roddick—founder of The Body Shop. She cares deeply for the environment, the Third World, and offering customers a range of efficacious products, many based on traditional wisdom. Her profound commitment can make her sometimes appear stubborn, irascible, and pugnacious—attributes that rein-force followers' beliefs that she really means business. What started as a potential weakness has become a strength.

The reason for this inevitable connection between leadership and personal risk is complex. It begins with an understanding that leadership is for a purpose. There is some superordinate desired end state, which energizes the leader who in turn gives energy to followers. Effective leaders really *care* about this goal. They care enough to reveal their authentic selves.

The verb *to care* is significant here. In English, *care* is a soft word, but we all know, sometimes through bitter experience, that really caring is one of the hardest things we ever do. When we show what we care about, we become vulnerable. It is this vulnerability that entails personal risk. The capacity to do this means leaders are prepared to use their passions to stretch the performance of others and to challenge established organizational dogma. Inevitably, though, the outcomes are uncertain.

We label this kind of caring "tough empathy." It means leaders never lose sight of what they are there to do. They give people what they *need* rather than what they *want.* They never forget the task and the purpose as well as the people.[3]

Tough empathy goes far beyond the polite concern for the team that some managers express as they return fresh from their latest interpersonal skills training program. It is an outcome of really caring that balances respect for the individual, the task at hand, and the shared higher purpose. It is confirmation that the leader is doing more than simply playing a role: he or she is living up to the obligations of the job.

Let's take another example. Alain Levy was previously the CEO of PolyGram Music and is now the boss of EMI Music. When Alain first joined PolyGram as head of its French operations, he came across as rather aloof and intellectual. His forte is numbers, which speak to him in subtle tones most managers never hear. His juniors soon spread the word that if they went to a meeting with Levy and didn't know every single pertinent figure, they would be in for a difficult time. Though effective with small groups, Levy is ill at ease in front of large audiences. He is blunt and amiably profane, with an iconoclastic distaste for hierarchy that appeals instantly to creative people. He often disarms his critics by displaying those traits along with some of the musical expertise he learned while working with CBS in the United States.

On one occasion, he chose to help a group of young executives select which single to release first from an album. In the music industry this is a critical task, since a single tune can spell success or failure for the project. It's usually a noisy job, with a good deal of heated debate. This session was no exception. Soon, Levy's voice cut through the clamor. "You bloody idiots! You don't know what the hell you're talking about. We always have a dance track first!" Within twenty-four hours, the story spread throughout the organization. It was the best internal publicity Levy ever got. Word spread that he was a no-nonsense, down-to-earth leader who had mastered his craft. "Levy really knows how to pick singles," people said. He had shown that he had a real feel for the business and cared enough about it to reveal his own powerful emotions.

The people who work with Alain Levy continue to admire and rely on his strengths in his current role at EMI, and they accept his weaknesses. In fact, we might even go so far as to suggest that they are attracted by his ferocity of purpose. This is tough empathy at work. Alain Levy, like John Latham, is not an insensitive man. He understands the impact of his sometimes blunt and emotional style. But he also knows that in showing who he is, there will inevitably be both rough and smooth, light and dark.

Passion Plays

Another exemplar of tough empathy is Sir Richard Sykes, the rector of Imperial College at the University of London. Sykes is a scientist who made his career at Glaxo Wellcome (which later became GlaxoSmithKline), culminating in several very successful years as its chairman. Sykes is well known for his passion and energy—as well as his anger and irritability. When heading the R&D division at Glaxo, he gave a year-end review to the senior scientists at the company, and one of the authors was present. At the end, one of the researchers questioned him on the company's new compounds, and the two engaged in a short but heated debate. Questions and answers were taken from others for a further twenty minutes before the researcher came back to the subject once more. "Dr. Sykes," he began, "you still fail to understand the structure of the new compound." Sykes's rising temper was visible as he marched to the back of the room and, before the assembled research expertise of the entire company, yelled, "All right, lad, let's have a look at your notes!" There and then, the two of them sorted out their differences.

For some, this public display of temper may seem an inappropriate weakness. But of course, it also communicates powerfully his deep belief in the discussion of basic science—a core organizational, as well as personal, value. Sykes really cared—so much, he was prepared to get angry. The point was reinforced by the following incident told to us by one of his followers. Dr. Sykes showed a similar audience of highly intelligent scientists a strand of DNA. He indicated the area thought to be responsible for a serious disease—

simply and directly he announced a commitment to find a cure. Some in the room were reduced to tears. For all the force of his temper, his followers never doubted his absolute commitment to the overarching purpose of the company.

Why Leadership Means Risk

Which vulnerable areas are revealed, and how, often reveals the real skill of a leader—and this is a theme to which we will return. But for the moment let's return to the question *why*? What is it that drives individuals to take these kinds of personal risks?

Some years ago, drawing upon the distinction originally identified by James McGregor Burns between transactional and transformational leadership, Alistair Mant contrasted two modes of thought: the binary and the ternary. In the first, individuals are driven to control, dominate, or seduce others in the interests of personal survival. In the second, interpersonal power is regulated to some extent by a *third corner*—an idea, a purpose, or an institution that defines what life is about. "Their instinct is to ask not, 'Shall I win?' but rather, 'What's it for?'" Mant explained. "These people . . . make good leaders precisely because they are not badgered by threats to survival. From the vantage point, or haven, of the 'third corner' they can run personal risks in the pursuit of some higher purpose and observe themselves, as from a great height, in their own interpersonal relationships. They can, in short, see the joke, which means they are capable of thinking at two levels of abstraction at the same time."[4]

Mant's observations mirror our experience. Great leaders are driven by an unbending sense of purpose—and it is this that impels them to take personal risks. As yachtsman Pete Goss put it. "You are there to serve a purpose. The boat isn't there to get you round the world. You are there to get the boat round the world. It's about stewardship."

The effects of this, to an extent, create a curious paradox. In showing that they really care about something, leaders will inevitably reveal something of their true selves. Others will see that they are not simply playing a role or living up to the minimum obligations of their jobs. Such displays of authenticity are an essential precondition for leadership. Yet, at the same time, leaders must retain an awareness of their own performance, the impact of their actions on others, the extent to which their higher purpose is, or is not, advanced. As noted, this requires a certain sense of detachment or role distance—in Mant's terms, an ability to see the joke.

John Latham, Alain Levy, Richard Sykes, Pete Goss—none of these leaders ever forget why they are there. They are there to give people what they *need* rather than what they *want*. They communicate a tough empathy that balances respect for the individual, the task at hand, and, ultimately, the higher purpose.

This is a difficult balancing act—and the personal costs are often higher for the leader than the led. "Some theories of leadership make caring look effortless. It isn't," Paulanne Mancuso, then president and CEO of Calvin Klein Cosmetics, told us. "You have to do things you don't want to do, and that's hard." Or as the Nestlé boss, Peter Brabeck, confided, "You have to be emotionally honest in relationships—you get to the edge. You cannot worry that this person might have been something to you in your life. There comes a point where what you are trying to achieve is bigger than the person. It's not that you want it, but some situations demand it."

R-E-S-P-E-C-T

Leaders put themselves on the line, take personal risks, in an array of challenging settings. They risk themselves and thereby earn respect. One of the leaders we encountered was Paul McDermott, the manager of an infamous public housing estate in an American inner city. The estate had witnessed tragic and brutal murders and prolonged rioting in the 1980s. Now, thanks to enormous effort and persistence, the estate attracts delegations from around the world excited by its transformation. Paul, a tough and articulate Irish American, has been at the heart of the changes. In order to have an impact on the estate, he has built around himself a strong team of talented individuals, leaders in their own right. To do this he is, as he puts it, always honest with people. He believes that you cannot develop relations of respect without honesty. *Respect* is one of his favorite words, and he wins it by putting himself on the line—with unswerving commitment to improving the lives and the community of the tenants. And he insists that winning respect is not a one-off event but a never-ending process.

There are many examples of Paul earning respect. Early on, he decided to move the estate offices away from the safer periphery of the estate right into the middle. To do this, he had to literally move out the crack dealers, who did not, of course, respond kindly. What's more, in the face of threats, he insisted he and his team stay at the center of things: "We need to show everybody that we mean business." Paul is so concerned about the tenants he works with that he has obstinately ignored all our career advice that it is time for him to move on. He says he works in one of the most exciting places around, with people he cares deeply about and who respect him. He even has fun. It may be tough, but he really cares.

Another up-front leader is Greg Dyke. When he took over at the BBC, his commercial rivals were spending substantially more on programs than the BBC was. Dyke knew that in order to survive in a competitive digital world, the BBC needed to increase its expenditure on program making. He communicated this openly and directly to his staff and, having secured their buy-in, began to restructure the organization. Although some employees lost their jobs, he was able to maintain people's commitment. "Once you have people with you," he says, "you can make the difficult decisions that need to be made."[5]

While Dyke did galvanize the staff, increase morale, and bring creative program making back to the heart of the BBC, he also made enemies, some of them powerful. There were those, just off-stage, waiting for and wanting him to make mistakes. When he did, he was vulnerable and exposed—and they swooped. Dyke lost his job. Authentic leadership is a dangerous game. No one should think otherwise.

The Art of Revelation

Cynics might suggest that many of the people we are citing have reached powerful positions and can afford to express themselves with less fear of reprisal. Greg Dyke is a wealthy man; he can afford to be himself. The reality is that most of these leaders developed this level of commitment at a much earlier stage in their working lives. They didn't save it all up until they reached the top. Think about it: is it possible to withhold self-expression and personal values for much of your career and then suddenly open up? It seems an unlikely behavioral trick. When individuals wait before expressing their real selves, they often find that by the time they have reached the position they aspire to, they have lost the capacity for both self-awareness and self-disclosure.

At the most basic level, the barrier that limits self-expression and strong personal commitment typically lies within. Many people are prevented from risk taking by their own personal defensiveness. This requires some explanation. Psychologists argue, convincingly, that despite the different roles that each of us plays in day-to-day life—father, mother, son, daughter, husband, manager, tennis club member, neighborhood committee chairman, and so on—there is underneath a basic self-concept that holds these various perform-ances together.[6] It is our own conception of "who we are."

Some of this self is publicly revealed. Think for a moment of the person who introduces herself as "athletic" or "creative." Occasion-ally, this is a genuine attempt to openly share with others a sense of what may be a common thread running between the differing role performances played out in day-to-day life.

But much of the self-concept is private—shared only at inti-mate moments with close friends or family, or sometimes not at all. And because our self-concept is valuable, it is highly defended. Those who appear to come too close to it or to attack it are met with a rich and varied array of defense mechanisms. Indicate to some-one, for example, that you feel they are disorganized and late for meetings, and you may be met with angry denial, swift "agreement," or even an attempt to laugh it off as a joke. All three responses—not just the first—can be interpreted as defensive responses that, in effect, are a sign of rejecting the message. You may have noticed how often the "wrong" behavior persists long after you thought your message had been delivered. The reality most often is that your message hit the defensive barrier and bounced away—it was never really received.

In varying degrees, all of us display defensiveness. We limit the extent to which we reveal ourselves to others or take on board their feedback. Leaders have defense mechanisms, too, of course. Our argument is certainly not that they are distinguished by "revealing all" indiscriminately. Rather, it is that these leaders show enough for others to see the contours of a real person, some of whose qualities may be attractive or exciting to them. In other words, they reveal enough—skillfully. Many other people simply don't get to first base; they don't reveal enough. There are a number of reasons for this.

First, at the top of most organizations, introverts are overrepresented.[7] If you are less motivated to interact with others—as introverts are—then you will have fewer opportunities, and less energy, for showing others who you are. Unfortunately, most of the leadership and management recipe books seem to overlook this point. They assume that we are all extroverts. Management by wandering about—MBWA, as it was known—may have seemed obvious to extroverts, but to introverts it was a major (and rather challenging) revelation. We have worked for years with senior executives who, when receiving feedback from 360-degree (peers, bosses, and subordinates) questionnaires, express amazement when they discover that their colleagues seem unsure of who they are or what they stand for.

Second, the knowledge economy has produced increasing ranks of technical or knowledge specialists, relatively few of whom demonstrate the interpersonal attributes required for leadership. Indeed, in our experience, it is in knowledge-intensive firms where the shortage of leadership capability is most acutely felt. Why is this? We believe it is largely because these individuals are oriented neither to relationships with their colleagues nor to their shared tasks—but instead to their areas of specialist expertise, whatever they may be.

We have worked, for example, in beer companies and found individuals obsessed with foam stability. In food companies, we have met fatty-acid specialists. In pharmaceutical businesses, there are individuals whose major life interest is vomit centers. And in investment banks, there are financial-derivative experts. Very few of these technicians seem keen to leave their specialist comfort zones to deal with the messy business of leading others. Why should they? Many have built their careers around their specialist expertise, are handsomely rewarded for their talents, and enjoy jobs with high degrees of discretion and personal challenge. Insofar as they wish to be known, it is for their expertise rather than their individual differences, or personal idiosyncrasies. In their world, the winners are the most expert; and if you have expertise, many would argue, you do not need to be led.

Finally, there is another population—middle managers and operatives in the main—who have been squeezed by the organizational changes of the past twenty years. Delayering, downsizing, reengineering, and so on have taken their toll. As organizations have restructured, many of these individuals have been asked to work harder and longer, have had their work performance more precisely monitored and measured, and have seen their career structures (such as they were) collapse.[8]

This (often unilateral) renegotiation of the psychological contract has produced not empowerment but a sense of cynicism, betrayal, and mistrust. In this climate, individuals are unlikely to display the commitment and personal risk taking required for effective leadership. Rather, as a matter of personal survival, individuals are likely to look after themselves by reducing their commitment at work and reserving their real energies for their private lives. These are the reluctant managers who, under increasing pressure at work, save their real selves for family, leisure, and personal pursuits.[9] They rarely have the stomach for leadership at work.

We have painted a deliberately bleak picture. Not all organizations or workplaces are dominated by introverted senior executives, specialist technicians, alienated middle managers, and cynical operatives. Some organizations have excellent people management practices and have worked hard to empower their employees and develop their leadership capabilities. These are the ones sometimes cited in the business press, though it is somewhat depressing to note just how much of our business reporting continues to ignore the significance of people practices. But for each of these celebrated cases, we suspect there are many others where it may be increasingly tough for individuals to follow our maxim: Take personal risks! Reveal your weaknesses!

This ability to take personal risks is not restricted to those at or near the top of hierarchies. There are leaders in many places in really effective organizations. While researching this book, we have interviewed and observed nurses, teachers, and junior state officials, many of whom have been willing to lay a little of themselves on the line every day; and by skillfully revealing their weaknesses, they have made these weaknesses work for them.

Leaders with Purpose

So what can be done? The answers begin with you. *Unless you are clear about your purpose and your values and are doing something that you really care about, it is difficult to act as a leader.* You are unlikely to possess the will and the resilience that are needed to carry you through the inevitable uncertainties and setbacks. It is hard to see how a sense of purpose or personal values can be taught in any conventional sense—although we are sure that through skillful coaching, mentoring, and confidence-building experiences, individuals can come to a better appreciation of who they are and what they want. However, we remain stubbornly convinced of the significance of meaningful work for healthy individuals and for cohesive societies.

As Studs Terkel puts it unforgettably in his book *Working*, "Work is about daily meaning as well as daily bread; for recognition as well as cash; in short, for a sort of life rather than a Monday-through-Friday sort of dying . . . We have a right to ask of work that it include meaning, recognition, astonishment and life."[10]

Is this sense of purpose, caring enough to reveal personal weakness, sufficient to make individuals good leaders? No—but it is an important foundation. The next step is to consider more fully the relational aspect of leadership, for as we suggested earlier, leaders reveal enough—and skillfully.

What does this mean in practice? First, it does not mean that leaders reveal all their personal weaknesses. Not only is this impractical (we are unlikely to know all our weaknesses), but it is also asking too much. After all, if you are aware of every flaw in another person, this is likely to destroy rather than enhance their leadership credibility. In effect, their weaknesses will drown out their strengths.[11]

So, good leaders focus dissatisfaction. As with the personal differences, they transform into leadership assets, so the weaknesses they reveal are *real* and *perceived*. But in addition, these weaknesses are not fatal flaws; they show how others may help; and above all, they are humanity confirming. Let's take each of these qualities in turn.

First, authentic leaders emphatically do not invent mock weaknesses to distract attention from the real ones. This lack of authenticity is swiftly spotted by others. If you have ever interviewed someone, asked them to report their weaknesses, and heard them piously reply, "I am a little too ambitious," or "I expect too much of others," then you will have witnessed at first hand the doomed attempt to serve up (yet another) strength as a so-called weakness.

Nor does it wash if individuals try to cover underlying weaknesses with a fake alternative. Think, for example, of how you might react to someone who pleads absentmindedness to cover inconsistency or lies.

So for weaknesses to "work," they must be real. But if a real weakness is central to task performance, then this will most likely be a fatal flaw. The new head of the accounting department is unlikely to gain much credit if she announces that she never did quite understand discounted cash flow. Pete Goss is unlikely to attract members to his sailing team if he reveals that he has no head for navigation. This is where we have to be careful about the contexts within which it might be possible to display leadership—some places simply won't work for us.

At the extremes, it is easy to spot fatal flaws, but in reality, the day-to-day judgments are much finer. For a human resources director, for instance, gossip can be seen as a fatal flaw, since her privileged position depends on guarding the information it gives her. But this is something of a paradox, since she must trade information to get people to open up to her. The solution is to let out the right kind of inside information—not betraying personal confidences ("Susie is never going to be promoted"), but perhaps giving an advance hint about a coming increase in benefits.

Knowing which weaknesses to reveal, and when, is often a highly honed art closely linked to the ability to sense the requirements of different situations—a theme we address in detail in the next chapter. For example, while coach of the Newcastle United, Barcelona, and England soccer teams, the well-traveled veteran, Sir Bobby Robson, developed a reputation for confusing or completely forgetting players' names. Few leaders would be able to survive this potentially fatal, basic error. But Robson was able to craft this weakness around his love for the game of soccer. His players indulged him—as they would an elderly, eccentric professor—and Robson learned to use his forgetfulness as a mischievous source of locker-room humor.

Here, then, is a weakness working for a leader—confirming, through personal foibles, their humanity. And it is this humanity-enhancing quality that is the most important reason why aspiring leaders must learn to be comfortable with at least some of their areas of incompetence and personal weakness. In effect, weaknesses reveal that a person is present—not a mere role holder. Think, for example, of the abiding popular affection for President John F. Kennedy, Muhammad Ali, and Princess Diana. All exhibited, in fairly public fashion, human weaknesses for which we forgave them. All showed enough for us to see that they might be more than, respectively, just another politician, sportsman, or member of royalty. All remain with their reputations largely intact.

Take President Kennedy. Ask any group of people to identify his weaknesses. In our experience, they will unerringly speak of him as a womanizer—some with envy and some with moral condemnation. The truth is that, by all accounts, he was a fairly indiscreet womanizer. The revelation of this weakness has, through the generations, effectively served to divert attention from many other possible flaws.

Revealing a weakness can also show others how they can help. In effect, it can build solidarity between leader and led. Offering "I am badly organized" signals to an assistant that the leader needs help with their diary. "I don't have the technical knowledge" shows a colleague that their expertise is important for the team.

Bill Burns at Roche admits that when a quick decision is needed, he often puts it off. "Occasionally, I get too involved in the detail—and some say I am too soft—not prepared to make the hard decisions." But Burns often uses his procrastination to teach initiative and independence: "I am trying to get others to make decisions."

Similarly, we know a magazine editor in New York who cheerfully confesses that he's color blind in the red/green spectrum, and leaves all decisions on colors to his art staff. They are all the more empowered; they will argue hotly over small nuances, knowing that they can't blame the editor for a bad choice.

There is, paradoxically, a feel-good factor in taking the initiative in revealing weakness. Leaders feel better because rather than having their weaknesses revealed by others—and so feeling defensive and inadequate—they have "owned up" first. (This also prevents colleagues from inventing potentially more damaging weaknesses!) And followers feel better because they have been given something that they can legitimately and publicly complain about (rather than privately and vindictively). It is an organizational wailing wall.

When we discuss owning up to weakness with those we work with, the benefits are not hard to demonstrate. Individuals can quickly grasp the leadership advantages. But as we have already discussed, there are organizational pressures that work against this, and management development processes that seem to celebrate the pursuit of perfection and individual advantage rather than skillful leadership.

Clearly, elite individual performance—in sports, the arts, or science, for example—may involve the attempt to have individuals get as near perfect as possible. But this is rarely a basis for leadership. Proving that you are better—or even the best—is appropriate for individually competitive, but not cooperative, contexts. Top business schools are good at developing the analytical skills required for consultants, advisers, and strategists, but there seems to be a gap in their ability to develop leadership.

Caveats and Pickles

We are not arguing that leadership is built primarily around individual weakness. That would be a naïve proposition. Clearly, weaknesses are best revealed after showing your strengths, are rarely helpful in a crisis, and typically should be exposed sparingly. At the BBC, for instance, Greg Dyke occasionally let his hot temper erupt. Later he always called the luckless target of his wrath to apologize. But this obviously can't become a daily performance, or anything like it. Shown too often, a weakness becomes a defining characteristic, not a tolerable exception. Dyke is selective in using his temper to best effect.

Nor are we claiming that some weaknesses cannot and shouldn't be addressed, minimized, and sometimes eliminated. That would be a charter for complacency and minimal personal development.

But we are claiming that personal risks and the revelation of weakness are an inevitable concomitant of a strong sense of purpose and really caring. And that effective leaders come to understand the ways in which they can best express their shortcomings— knowing that others will talk about them. When we interviewed John Latham's colleagues about him, for example, it was striking how candidly they talked to strangers with a tape recorder about his weaknesses—by no means maliciously, but very frankly. They knew he wouldn't mind.

In fact, in most cases, displaying weakness should be more show than talk. One memorable showing of a forgivable weakness can become part of a leader's legend, told and retold by the followers.

Greg Dyke created a moment like that at a Christmas lunch for his BBC leadership group. This was a group of about eighty BBC executives created by him to address the problems of an organization he believed to be overmanaged and underled. The lunch was at a theater, the home of the Magic Circle, with a professional magician who performed brilliantly. Then Dyke himself performed a trick he had learned, laboriously. With fingers like sausages, he is far from dexterous, and did the trick badly, to the howls of his staff. He never had to show his clumsiness again; the story is affectionately remembered to this day.

Did Greg Dyke deliberately set out to reveal a weakness—in this case, a lack of manual dexterity? Of course not. But we suspect that Greg knows that being human makes him a better leader. Of course, he also knows what business he is in: entertainment. Attempting some magic combines marvelous situation sensing, revelation of weakness (in this case, funny, minor, and tolerable), and an ability to identify with and get close to his colleagues. It was a master class not in magic, but in the magic of leadership.

At the outset of this chapter, we argued that leaders who really care will inevitably expose personal strengths and weaknesses. As we completed this book, a well-known, now retired English soccer coach, Brian Clough, died. His major achievements were to take two unfashionable English teams—Derby County and Nottingham Forest—and transform them into English champions. Extraordinarily, given a modestly talented squad and limited resources, Forest went on to win the fiercely competitive European championship twice in consecutive years.

Clearly, Clough passes our base test as a leader. He was able to excite (average) players to higher levels of performance. How did he do it? Perhaps not surprisingly, the tributes and obituaries focused on Clough's exceptional "player management"—he was described as "unique," "extraordinary," "maverick," and "charismatic."

How were these qualities communicated to the players? One of them, John Robertson, "transformed from an overweight slacker into an established international," said, "Clough never missed a trick. Every piece of advice he gave me was spot on . . . it helped that I was in awe of him . . . for three or four years I couldn't wait for Saturdays . . . I *wanted* to play for him."[12]

Another, Martin O'Neill, described in Clough's own autobiography as "a good player but a pain in the arse," said, "He was egocentric, sometimes a bully, often impossible, but I wouldn't have missed a moment of being managed by him, because as a manager, he was magical."[13]

The broadcaster and journalist Michael Parkinson wrote of Clough, "He was fond of saying, 'I'm a big head. Not a figurehead'. In fact he was both. He was also loveable and impossible, wise and silly, attractive and appalling. He was a pickle of a man."[14]

Did Brian Clough really care? Yes. He cared about winning. He cared about winning the right way—his teams were drilled to play a skillful, passing game; players were punished if they argued with referees. He cared about discipline—demanding high standards of dress and appearance from players. He cared about education—insisting young players completed their college studies. He cared about social justice—during the miners' strike in the 1980s, he opened turnstiles to the strikers and let them in free.

Did these strong passions reveal strengths and weaknesses? Yes. He was a "pickle." Players were in awe of him and loved him. He was a mix, as many observed, between a regimental sergeant major and an elder brother. He absolutely displayed tough empathy.

Did Clough knowingly play to these strengths and weaknesses? Yes. When awarded the OBE, he claimed that it must stand for "Old Big 'Ead." Granted the freedom of the City of Nottingham, he spoke of his fondness for the River Trent flowing through it and remarked, "[It's] lovely. I know because I have walked on it for 18 years!" Asked if he was the best manager ever, he replied, "No, but I am probably in the top one."[15]

Brian Clough was a marvelous example of an individual unashamed to let his self shine through—warts and all. In the process, he took risks—and he paid for them. His outspoken character meant he would never achieve the England manager role that he coveted. His alcoholism (barely concealed) eventually overtook him and blighted the later stages of his career. But his reputation as a great leader remains intact.

The most skillful leaders can actually make their weaknesses work for them—revealing their humanity and moving them beyond just the excellent role player. But they must do this with skill and, critically, in context. In the next chapter, we examine the ways in which leaders read the context in which they must operate, how they develop an understanding of the real limits to their actions. We also examine how truly effective leaders both read and rewrite the contexts. This requires an understanding of that which can be changed—and that which cannot.

FOUR

Read—and Rewrite—
the Context

T HE EXERCISE OF LEADERSHIP is contextual. Always. This undermines the notion of a universal leadership formula. Effective leaders understand that there are no universals, no guaranteed ways of ensuring your leadership impact. On the contrary, they practice and hone their context-reading skills and realistically appraise their ability to rewrite that context.[1]

In the next two chapters, we will explore and illustrate just how leaders do this. We begin by examining the immediate context of the leader: the individuals and teams they interact with on a regular basis. This notion is captured in some formulations of emotional intelligence.[2] For example, Richard Boyatzis refers to a cluster of competences around the notion of social capability—among them, influencing, teamwork, and conflict management.[3] In chapter 5, we extend this idea to show that effective leaders need understanding of the wider organizational context beyond the immediate group of people with whom they regularly interact. And we will go on to consider the critical importance of this aspect of leadership.

Our starting point is a simple, undeniable observation: human actions—whether involving leadership or not—do not take place in a vacuum. They are conditioned by the social realities in which individuals act. These social realities form an important part of the context. They can be no more wished away than can gravity. Effective leadership involves recognizing the limitations of context as well as the potential opportunities. Skillful leaders are realists. They have a well-developed sense of what can be changed—and what cannot. They understand the real conditions in which they must operate, and work within those constraints.[4]

The notion that leadership is dependent on context is not new. Many years ago the sociologist George Homans memorably observed:

> There are no rules for human behavior that apply in every situation without limit or change. Humanity yearns for certainty; it has looked for such rules for thousands of years but has not found them. For every principle it has discovered, it has also discovered a conflict of principles. In recent years men of practical affairs—industrial executives, for instance—have often come to psychologists and sociologists begging for a plan or set of rules that the executives can apply "across the board"— that is, in all circumstances—in dealing with their employees. There are no such rules, and if there were, they would be dangerous. They might work well for a time; then changing circumstances would make them inappropriate, and the leader would

have to deal with a new situation while his mind was clogged with old rules. The maxims of leadership we shall state are, therefore, not to be taken as absolutes but only as convenient guides for the behavior of a leader. They apply only within limits determined by the situation that faces him, and there are situations where the maxims will conflict with one another. What a leader needs to have is not a set of rules but a good method of analyzing the situation in which he must act. If the analysis is adequate, a way of dealing with the situation will suggest itself. And if, as a working guide, the leader does have some simple rules in mind, analysis will show him where their limits lie.[5]

It's One-on-One

If context is critical, being sensitive to that context, being able to detect the way the wind is blowing, is essential for any leader. Authentic leaders have good, sometimes excellent, situation-sensing capabilities.

Like many successful leaders, Patti Cazzato learned situation sensing from her experience as a sales representative. She put this to good use in her subsequent career as a senior vice president at Gap. Early experience of the sales encounter is cited by many leaders as highly influential in developing situation sensing. "Being in sales was the best thing, because it forced me to deal with many different types of people, and put me into situations when I was young and, quite honestly, fearful. I had to deal with a lot of older men, who were established general managers in department stores. It made me think before I spoke, assess my audience, and learn to communicate with different people in different ways," Cazzato told us.

Having learned the skill, Cazzato uses it and helps others to do so. "I ask a lot of questions," she said. "I check regularly with the field, my customers, regional managers, directors of stores. Even if they don't report to me, I always check in to ask, 'What's going on?'" And she trains her team to do likewise so that everyone is tuned in to the pulse of the Gap organization. "Some of my employees needed to understand the big picture better," she told us. "I want them to be more in touch with their employees and their customers. I am trying to build a new kind of organization."

Perhaps what is most significant about the sales experience is that it involves many one-to-one encounters. As another of our respondents tellingly remarked, "In the end, business is one-to-one."

Experiences out of the comfort zone may also heighten situation-sensing capability. Peter Brabeck says he first learned the skill during his military service in Austria at the age of seventeen. He found himself closely observing his own and others' reactions to their barely tolerable living conditions and inhumane treatment. Some attempted suicide, others accommodated, still others showed no reaction, while some grew comfortable with the poor treatment. For the first time, Brabeck was in a position to benefit from situation sensing. The more he could learn about his superior officers and their plans, the more he could anticipate their behavior and, hence, stay out of their way. For Brabeck, understanding that link gave birth to insight.

John Bowmer, former chairman and CEO of California-headquartered global employment firm Adecco, cites living in a school camp in Western Nigeria as an experience that stimulated his situation-sensing capacity. He learned from the complex negotiation of relationships between the missionaries based at the school and the indigenous population. In all of these experiences far from the leaders' comfort zones, the initial feeling is of not understanding at all what is going on. For many, that feeling triggers enhanced situation sensing.

What Does Situation Sensing Involve?

There are three separate, but related, elements to effective situation sensing. The first is made up of observational and cognitive skills. Leaders see and sense what's going on in their organizations—and then use their cognitive skills to interpret these observations. They pick up and interpret soft data, sometimes without any verbal explanation. They know when team morale is shaky or when complacency needs challenging. They collect information, seemingly through osmosis, and use it to understand the context in which they are aspiring to lead.

The process is subtle—so much so that it is not always easy to "see" it. But there are some key moments where you may often observe this skill—or its absence—in workplace interactions. Think of meetings, for example, when someone joins late and then acts like a bull in a china shop. This kind of disruption typically reflects "negative" situation sensing. Others seem to be able to join a meeting and immediately tune in, effortlessly picking up on atmosphere or ambience.

You will also see this skill when deals are being done. There will always come a point during merger or acquisition negotiations, for instance, when all the numbers have been run, but the vital determining factor will be the leader's sense of whether it "feels right" to proceed. Those who make the right call have good situation-sensing capabilities.

Highly task-oriented executives very often neglect the basic observational work. They rush into action before fully understanding the situation—sometimes with very negative consequences. As we show later, there are useful observational frameworks that can help individuals to develop awareness of this skill and start to practice it.

The second element of situation sensing is made up of behavioral and adaptive skills. Having observed and understood the situation, effective leaders adjust their behaviors. They adapt without ever losing their sense of self. They are what we call *authentic chameleons*. The chameleon adapts dramatically to its environment or context without ever ceasing to be a chameleon. For leaders, this behavioral element of situation sensing involves the self-conscious use of social skills to maximize their leadership impact in a particular context. These individuals are able to use a wide range of behaviors: they can create both closeness and distance; leverage their strengths but reveal their human weaknesses; move fast but seem to be in control of time.

Think, for example, of the skillful interventions of Rudy Giuliani, former mayor of New York City. During the traumatic hours and days immediately following 9/11, Giuliani sensed that, as a leader, he needed to be out on the streets, with the people. He tuned in to the context. Compare this with the immediate actions of President Bush: first—memorably captured in Michael Moore's film *Fahrenheit 9/11*—visibly frozen for several minutes on stage during a school visit at the time of the attacks; then, hidden from view, out of contact, somewhere in the skies over the United States with armed protection.

Arguably, President Bush's primary leadership responsibility was to ensure the executive chain of command—by remaining out of harm's way. Yet, his actions made him appear distant and out of touch. By contrast, Giuliani's situation sensing was more immediate and addressed the emotional needs of his followers. New Yorkers were in harm's way, and Giuliani showed that he was with them. At a time of terrible anguish, he gave them a sense of pride in themselves and their city that helped them cope. (In doing so, he also began to rewrite the context—the next point.)

The final element of effective situation sensing is that leaders use their own behavior to change the situation. They exemplify an alternative context. When Greg Dyke arrived at the BBC, he was shocked by the number of unhappy people he encountered. His response was to model a more positive, energized vision for the organization. By personifying a new style, he was attempting to change the context. He was himself—cheerful and positive—talking to people in the corridor, communicating excitement about new shows or upcoming dramas. Dyke tried to change the somewhat austere atmosphere of the BBC executive meetings. He knew he had succeeded when a group of senior executives summoned to the boardroom heard laughter inside and assumed they had gone to the wrong room.

The lesson is that leaders are not passive recipients of the context. On the contrary, they work with their followers to socially construct an alternative reality.[6] This capacity is what differentiates those who merely react to situations from those who have the capacity to transform them.

Leaders know that situation sensing is important. They also know that it becomes more critical as you move up organizational hierarchies. Elevation brings with it increasingly sanitized information—filtered through the eyes and ears of others who may have a view about what the leader should know. As you get nearer to the top, you receive more information, but it can become less reliable. As John Bowmer explains, "If you are successful, you are held more and more in awe, and, as a result you get less and less honest information."

Authentic leaders know this and take steps to ensure they remain connected to the action, sensitive to the ever-changing context.

Senses Working Overtime

Let's examine a couple of examples of situation sensing in more detail. Greg Dyke faced a situational challenge when he took over at the BBC. He had made his formidable reputation in the cutthroat world of commercial television, and here he was, leading a rather stuffy national institution. His early observations shocked him. When he offered a cheery "hello" in the elevator, his employees were inclined to look at their shoes. When he lunched in the cafeteria, space appeared around him. Even his senior colleagues seemed initially inclined to tell him what they thought he wanted to hear.

"It seemed a really strange place where people playacted the whole time," Dyke recalls. "No one was being themselves, because they didn't think that was allowed. Therefore, you had bright, interesting, and talented people being something completely different for no other reason than they thought they weren't allowed to be themselves."

Dyke decided to explore further and embarked on an extensive tour of the BBC's broadcasting empire. He visited local radio stations (often the unsung heroes of public-service broadcasting), science program units, drama shoots, the newsroom—always with a strictly no-red-carpet and no-entourage approach. He desperately did not want hierarchy to get in the way of understanding the context. He encountered a complex picture. At one level, morale was low, complaints were commonplace, cynicism excessive; and yet, when he probed a little deeper, he could sense creativity, innovation, and deep commitment to public-service broadcasting simmering beneath the surface.

Given his own high-energy, positive style, he found the cynicism depressing and energy-sapping. His leadership task in rewriting the context was to bring creativity, innovation, and commitment to the surface. And of course, his own behavior was crucial in making this happen.

Even the way in which Dyke started to make sense of the situation began to change it. Remember: no red carpet, no entourage—not a hint of the royal visit. Instead, as he began poking his nose into offices and studios, Dyke appeared as a friendly, sympathetic explorer. The more he came to understand the situation, the more he realized that in order to rewrite the context, he needed to win allies—to build constituencies of supporters—who would buy into his vision. Like the head teacher John Latham, Dyke asked, "What would make things work better around here?" Sometimes it was very small things: rewiring some sound equipment for a local radio station, or giving access to some garden space in overcrowded offices. "A lot of it was trivial—it would cost next to nothing," he told us. "By spending small amounts of money and changing a few things, you could win people over—gain their commitment."

But as he sensed, he was also adapting. One of the authors observed him at close hand as he came to terms with the traditions of the BBC. The corporation's grand council chamber is lined with portraits of previous director generals (all white, middle-aged men); the bust of Lord Reith, the organization's founder, stares down with frosty intensity. Here the director general endures interminable meetings with the BBC's governors—a curious mixture of regulators and cheerleaders. To all this Dyke displayed a shrewd and highly functional adaptation. For these occasions, his dress, demeanor,

and speech were toned down. He used formal modes of address—
especially to the chairman. Just occasionally, however, his irritation
showed: nervously snapping his spectacle case, he radiated impa-
tience with the speed of the governors' debates. Perhaps this is when
he began to make the enemies who would eventually undo him.

Symbolic Change

The first real changes Dyke introduced were symbolically significant in his attempt to rewrite the context. First, he phased out
the cars and chauffeurs assigned to each member of his executive
board. The chauffeurs were well treated, and the overall impact on
the program makers and support staff was very positive. In an
organization with a strong egalitarian aspiration, the long line of
expensive black cars parked outside its headquarters had been a
source of irritation, even alienation, for many staff.

Second, he cut the large budget spent on consultants. In one
year it went from £22 million to £3 million. This marked a radical
break from the previous regime and symbolized faith in the people
already inside the organization.

These symbols of change were combined with Dyke's manifest
commitment to the organization. Dyke really cared about the people he was leading, and the institution of which he was custodian.
One particularly poignant example demonstrates this. He had been
due to address staff from a very significant part of the BBC's operations: its regional and national teams, those who represent and
serve the interests of Scotland, Wales, Northern Ireland, and the
English regions. The night before the meeting, his house was destroyed by fire. Luckily, no one was hurt, but he was understand-
ably devastated. Yet Dyke still showed up. "I was absolutely wrecked,
and they could tell," he said, but his presence under these awful

circumstances was enormously appreciated. "What you've got to communicate," he observed, "is we value you. We value what you do."

Under Dyke, the BBC changed. Managers used to bulldozing their decisions through began to listen to their staff. Journalists who thought that their enemy was the sister news program down the hall—the morning news competing with lunchtime, and they with the evening broadcast—began (some would say only just) to look outside the organization to see what the real competition was doing.

There was a pattern to this change, a rhythm we see in other organizations with effective leaders. That rhythm is: observe, understand, adapt, and rewrite.

Rhythm King

Consider Rick Dobbis, an experienced senior executive in the music business with experience at companies such as RCA, Sony, and PolyGram. Rick is a quintessential New Yorker. We first observed him when he ran the PolyGram Labels Group, a loose association of PolyGram's smaller labels in the United States. He brought hard marketing expertise to this role, together with sensitivity to the more tender souls of the A&R world and, of course, to the artists. Then a new opportunity offered itself. He got the chance to run Poly-Gram's European operations—twenty-six countries accounting for around half of the group's profits.

Not many American entertainment executives make a successful transition to Europe (and the same is largely true of those who attempt the feat in the reverse direction). The contacts and cultures are fundamentally different. The situation-sensing challenges are enormous. The business covers large territories like France and Germany, both with distinctive musical cultures; medium-sized ones like Spain, with its potential to internationalize repertoire into

Latin America; Italy; Scandinavia, with a strongly emerging repertoire base; and smaller countries like Portugal and Belgium, which
rarely produce international hits but which still have thriving music
industries. (After all, it was a Belgian who invented the saxophone.)

Dobbis approached all of this contextual diversity with an endless cultural curiosity combined with a clearly communicated willingness to help. He avoided the "I know the best way to do this"
syndrome and conveyed a genuine openness to learn from his colleagues. He watched, understood, adapted, and, finally, began to
rewrite the context. He started to hold meetings of all sixteen managing directors. He ran workshops on best practice; he encouraged
the signing of local artists, always keeping close to the flavor of the
local music scene—resisting the temptation to impose from the
center. Gradually, almost imperceptibly, they formed into a strong
team. Repertoire flows between countries increased; the coordina-
tion of marketing international hits from the United States and the
United Kingdom improved. It became probably the strongest part
of PolyGram's operation.

As Rick Dobbis demonstrates, leadership works most effectively when you have understood the context and made a judgment
about what can be rewritten and what cannot.

Understanding Individuals

But what is it that leaders need to sense? Is there a way of cat-
egorizing the context to sharpen your situation-sensing skills? One
way of doing this is to consider three levels of analysis. First are the
key individuals who make the biggest impact on your performance.
Second are the important teams that you must be involved with to
get things done. And third are the organizational context and con-

straints within which you must operate. (We will return to the organizational context in chapter 5.)

Effective leaders recognize that understanding the critical individuals in their organization is a precondition for success. The motives, values, skills, and passions of their people are essential parts of the context. Successful leaders are relentlessly curious about their key people. They read the often subtle signals that people radiate that indicate their underlying motives, their critical competences, and, not least, their emotional state.

Some aspects are a little easier to understand. In general, assessing someone's technical competence—for example, to read a balance sheet, or write a marketing plan, or test the toxicity of a drug—is at least partly measurable. But getting a handle on motives and emotions is much harder. It's more instinctive and much more difficult to calibrate.

How can leaders collect this data? Our research and experience suggests there are some useful general principles. First, informal contexts are better than formal ones. An informal setting, such as a lunch, a hike, or a weekend picnic, helps both the leader and followers escape the boundaries imposed by the corporate structure. Whether the leader holds meetings in their office or in more relaxed settings, they need to choose the place that will feel the most comfortable for everyone and where they will not be interrupted.

Second, indirect evidence is better than asking up-front questions. If the leader asks a follower directly, "What are your key motives?" then the power relationship between them gets in the way of good data. The follower is inclined to produce the answer that he or she thinks the leader wants to hear. This also explains why when a leader is collecting motivational data, questions about the past are more useful than hypotheses about the future. "What did you most enjoy about your last assignment?" elicits better information than "Where do you see yourself in the next two years?"

Questions about events that have already occurred reveal what drove people's behavior at key moments in their lives. For younger people, this may involve critical moments in their education. For those with more developed job histories, the pattern of their choices can be most revealing. People who leave Apple after twelve months because they feel it is stiflingly bureaucratic almost certainly have very low structure motives (that is to say, their desire to make the world more predictable is not a primary motivator). For others, the pursuit of larger bonuses may be critical; or it might be the pursuit of more power or autonomy that drives choices.

It is not just work-related experiences that reveal underlying motives. Data from sporting and community activities can also be useful. Those with high-power drives often captain the golf club, become church wardens, or organize the local PTA. Others, driven by their motive for satisfying personal relationships, build teams around themselves and join informal associations. All of this data is collected, evaluated, and, of course, used by effective leaders.

There are also issues around time. "It takes time," John Bowmer told us. "As people begin to trust you, they reveal themselves more. That's how you get better at situation sensing. You begin to know the signs and develop a cadre of people who will tell you what people are worried about."

It is very important that the leader doesn't just pick up one clue and deduce a complete model of an individual's motives from it. Rather, they are constantly building up and adjusting their understanding of the key people around them. People are complicated, and we never know them completely. Exploring their underlying motives is always an approximation, but is vital for effective leadership.

Finally, and because of this complexity, we advise leaders to develop a network diagram of the individuals who have the biggest impact on their performance.[7] On it, they record their observations and intentions about motives and emotions. The diagram could include subordinates, bosses, peers, suppliers, customers, or partners. Any or each of these can make a big difference to leadership effectiveness. When carrying out this exercise, leaders must look for gaps—important individuals about whom they know very little. They could be in danger of making one of the biggest motivational mistakes of all: assuming that they are just like them.

This is a serious business, and the information needs to be synthesized and structured. While the process of gleaning data should feel relaxed, it should be recorded systematically so that the leader's diagram can be updated each time they get new input.

This data will help the leader—or would-be leader—assess what motivates each of the people surrounding him or her. This, in turn, makes it easier for the leader to enlist them in their cause. The idea, according to Roche's Bill Burns, is for the leader to show the followers how joining the cause will help them get what they want.

Effective leaders commit themselves to helping their people, discovering their real talents, and developing what Pete Goss calls "the giant within." In a similar vein, Nigel Morris, former COO of McLean, Virginia–headquartered Capital One, says, "I am helping people to achieve their dreams. I have a middle-of-the-year review where I deliberately ask how people are feeling. Not only day-to-day, but how they are growing, learning, and what bothers them. I am always trying to discover how I can add value to this person. I try to work backward from what they are good at and augment what they have."

This notion of working back from what people are good at is echoed by Bill Burns. He observes, along with many child psychologists, that "people have a defined personality by the age of four or five. If they are fundamentally introverted, don't try to turn them into a cheerleader."

Developing insight into motives, values, and emotions delivers leadership advantage, even in difficult circumstances. Consider the following example. When Ray van Schaik was chairman of Heineken in the early 1990s, those around him noted he had an almost magical situation-sensing ability. He was able to decipher the signals he received from colleagues and, most importantly, from Freddie Heineken, the third-generation family member and major shareholder who prided himself on being "always there without being there." While some senior managers wasted time trying to second-guess Heineken, van Schaik seemed to "just know" what Heineken wanted, despite their very different personalities.

Van Schaik was the intermediary—or shock absorber—between a charismatic and strong-willed family owner and the strong top executive team that he had been instrumental in assembling. Without world-class situation sensing, it could have been a disaster. Instead, under his stewardship, Heineken became positioned for major and continuing international growth.

Understanding individuals is not just an issue at the top of organizations. We interviewed a grill chef in a roadside café in Ohio. He told us how important it was to know just how each waitress would respond to the lunchtime rush. One needed very clear instructions; another, constant positive feedback; and yet another, to be left to sort it out for herself. We were equally impressed with a line supervisor at FedEx in Memphis, who knew exactly who could be relied on to track a complex package, and others who needed to be checked on carefully.

While collecting data on key individuals all over organizations is critical, it is not the whole picture. The most effective leaders also read and rewrite the complex and subtle dynamics of groups.

Understanding Groups

Because leadership is always an interplay between leader and led, the extensive research literature on group behavior is highly relevant to those who aspire to leadership roles.[8] Most often, they are not leading aggregates of individuals but groups and teams.

As with understanding individuals, knowing the groups you are leading is a continuous, never-ending process. A group is more than the sum of its members. It also consists of all the relationships among those members—the square of the number of the group—and thus the complex social structure of the group itself. As Bill Burns puts it, "You are sensing human nature. You need to think about people and culture, not just logic and the task. It's thinking about whether the group has its natural leader, or whether the appointed leader is not the natural leader. Then it's a matter of sensing whether there are difficulties or tensions, or mismatches within the group that need to be dealt with."

The trouble is that many aspiring leaders neglect groups and their dynamics. This is despite a rich body of knowledge that demonstrates the benefits of transforming loosely connected "groups" into high-performing "teams."[9]

Why does this happen? One explanation is that, particularly in Western cultures, we aren't trained to build teams. Except in team sports, schools and universities encourage us to compete, not collaborate. Problems are presented to individuals, and students are trained to be independent and not to ask for help.

In work organizations, teams come in many shapes and sizes. These range from the manager and his or her direct reports to cross-functional teams, task forces, and ad hoc problem-focused teams. Some leaders find their teams strung along the corridor beside them. Others find themselves running geographically dispersed teams spread across every continent.

Yet, despite this rich variation, there are some well-established basics of team behavior. Leaders with good situation-sensing skills seem to know this, either intuitively or through good training.

We have known for many years, for example, that high-performing teams tend to evolve toward a balance between two distinctive types of behavior. These behaviors are often referred to as task-related roles and maintenance, or relationship-related roles. Task roles are directly related to getting the job done. They include initiating activity, establishing targets, monitoring progress, organizing who does what, and so on. Under pressure in a team, these roles will always emerge first and will dominate. But unrestrained over time, the excessively task-focused team is likely to fragment. What holds a team together is the maintenance role. This is concerned with finding common ground between team members, mediating conflicts, and so on. But taken too far, the maintenance behaviors can also be damaging. An excess of them, and the team may enjoy each other's company but never get anything done.

When we discuss this distinction with Japanese executives, they take it as a self-evident truth that the most important thing a team does when it meets is to ensure that it meets again. In other words, for them, relationships start with maintenance. First we get to know each other—then we can do business. At Nissan in Japan, we met a first-line supervisor whose primary leadership principle was to make sure that he shared food and drink with his team every day. For him—and his followers—the maintenance aspects of his role were the platform for his leadership. This is in stark contrast to the United States, where relationships are more likely to begin with task—first we do business, then we get to know each other.

Good leaders are always sensitive to this subtle balance between task and maintenance behaviors and the current requirements of the team. They recognize that the balance is precarious and will shift according to the different requirements of the team. To some extent, this is almost a moment-by-moment process. Good leaders know when a decision must be made immediately, even when agreement has not been reached or when more time is needed to listen to others' views and search for consensus. For the longer term, they are also planning for how they might change the team's mix and composition as the tasks they face change.

Recycling Teams

When he took over as marketing director of the Barclays Group, the charismatic Simon Gulliford inherited a demoralized team. There was a low level of cooperation, some backstabbing, and a strong sense of cynicism about how far marketing could be developed at the bank. His first task, as he saw it, was to work on building them into a team that would come to see itself as the top marketing team in the financial services sector. He used all his considerable experience and talent at creating high-performance teams to move toward higher levels of cohesiveness and effectiveness. But of course, in the process, he was collecting data about the competences and motivations of particular individuals. When the right moment came, he had enough information on which to base some tough decisions. Some people were moved into new roles, yet others were moved out.

In effect, leaders recognize that teams pass through cycles of development and that the process can benefit from being managed.

These stages are sometimes referred to as forming (the team is put together), storming (there is conflict about what to do and how to do it), norming (some agreement is reached about how to work together), and performing (the team can now focus wholeheartedly on the task).

There is no inevitable progression between these four stages. For example, some teams simply disintegrate at the storming stage because of irresolvable differences between individuals; others, inappropriately, are excessively polite and try to avoid any kind of conflict. A major problem we increasingly see involves unrealistic attempts to demonstrate quick results. This often involves leaping straight from the forming to the performing stage—an ambition that ignores several decades of behavioral science research.

We sometimes see this in succession situations. For example, we observed a tough Mexican taking over the U.S. subsidiary of a major beverage company. His predecessor had built a strong team, but he had done so by building around opposition to the parent company. This created an us-and-them mentality. In order to change this, the new leader broke apart some well-formed and cohesive clans before moving on to build a new team for a different vision.

Adapting to Differ

Just as good leaders take time to understand individuals, they also pay attention to these subtle dimensions of team structure and process. And they understand that the work is continual. It is not just when two members leave and three join that a team is back to the "forming" stage. It more or less happens every time the team meets. Once again, the leader has to get the team settled before the real focus on performance can begin. This means building in time for people to relate to each other. This is a simple point but one that is often missed.

Bill Burns rarely makes this mistake. He invests his considerable facilitative skills in ensuring that his executive board colleagues can settle and interact in a way that suits the moment. How this happens varies between different colleagues and from meeting to meeting. Whether it is a quiet word in private, a timely joke to relieve tension, giving ground to let others air grievances, or pushing for closure at key moments, Bill has honed his skills to a high level, and his repertoire is extensive.

Working with him and his executive board at a team-building event, we noticed Bill quietly but firmly protecting a colleague under fire from some other members of the team; updating others on the private challenges faced by this individual during the coffee breaks (on which, of course, he was well informed); then revisiting the areas of concern in a low-key fashion to ensure closure toward the end of the meeting. Not unusually, our session overran a little— but it had achieved its purpose—and Bill had given another master class in subtle and skillful team facilitation.

Leaders like Bill Burns understand what they can bring to the team—and where they need help. In contrast, highly task-focused leaders, who need more maintenance-oriented team members to help hold it all together, are often the last people to recognize this. They are too concerned to get things started—and finished—to bother with the process. The more relationship-oriented leader tends, almost inevitably, to be more situation sensitive to the requirement for complementary task-focused colleagues.

Our work with leaders is often concentrated on helping highly task-focused individuals to recruit or develop people close to them with well-developed maintenance skills. Sometimes we need to encourage the maintenance-orientated leader to tolerate, even encourage, higher levels of cognitive conflict among the team. (This conflict—or creative tension—can be especially important for innovation.) Indeed, both kinds of leader need to understand the positive benefits of cognitive conflicts (the clash of ideas) and the potentially damaging consequences of affective conflict (when negative emotions make teams dysfunctional).[10]

Obviously, the more people there are on a team and the larger the number of possible interactions among them, the harder it is for a leader to know them, both as individuals and as a functioning group. The same is true if the team is highly diverse. Differences of race, religion, language, experience, and personal goals may slow the group's cohesiveness and make it harder to read.

In the short term, people who are similar usually find it easier to work with one another, have relationships that the leader can read, and form teams that bond quickly and produce results. Thus, it is tempting for a leader to build homogeneous teams. However, it has been shown that highly diverse groups, though they often under-perform homogeneous teams initially, can outperform in the longer term, once they have learned to cohere and take advantage of their wider range of experience and ideas. So if the task at hand is complex and will take some time, it may be better to opt for diversity.[11]

Issues of creativity and innovation are increasingly important. Organizations followed the fashionable advice of the 1990s to become mean, lean, delayered, and focused. But now they face a new question: how can we innovate given that everyone has become mean and focused? Creativity increases with diversity and declines with sameness. But the leader cannot run away from the challenges associated with increasing diversity. Again, situation-sensing skills are at a premium.

All Over the Place

Another leadership issue has emerged with the increasing pace of globalization. More and more leaders find themselves with teams in more than one location. These situations offer special leadership challenges. You cannot simply walk down the corridor for an informal chat, or go for a beer after work. How can leaders transcend these difficult circumstances?

Of course, they are aided by new modes of communication: e-mail, videoconferencing, and so on. But these are often not the panacea that the technologists would have us believe.[12] The reason is simple: human beings are hardwired for sociability.

In one example we encountered, a major pharmaceutical company decided to internationalize its R&D. It installed an excellent e-mail system and bought a cable under the Atlantic Ocean to facilitate videoconferencing. But within weeks, e-mail was branded as "evil mail," and videoconferencing became a recipe for increasing mistrust and negative politics. "What exactly were they saying as they moved away from the microphone?" "Are they passing notes to each other?" Far from speeding up the R&D process, these changes made things worse, mired in "flaming" (deliberately bombarding an individual with a barrage of e-mails) and other forms of miscommunication. The deteriorating situation was addressed by bringing the teams from either side of the Atlantic together face-to-face. Often, there was blood on the walls and ceilings, but at the end of four or five days together, they started to relate to each other as human beings and behave like effective teams.

On the basis of this (and many experiences like it), we now advise leaders with remote teams to first establish face-to-face relationships. Human beings are designed for such interaction.

Once face-to-face has been established, then relationships can be maintained by other means. (Consider the power of the humble letter—it doesn't all have to be high-tech.) It is not accidental that the financial districts of the world are geographically small—Wall Street, the City of London, the financial district of Tokyo—and after the close of trading, the bars and clubs are full of people socializing face-to-face. They are collecting data on each other.

When effective leaders of remote teams bring the team together, they intensify the social interactions. They appreciate that the team members need to get to know each other often quickly. The leader ensures that the team works hard, but then that they go to dinner together or to the theater—anywhere that enables the leader to collect data and to self-disclose. In such situations, leaders do not have time to slowly play themselves into the leadership role. Many introverts find this intensification very hard.

Finally, the costs of not establishing face-to-face relationships are greater than the costs of doing it. We give this advice so that you can arm yourself against the irate finance department checking your travel budget.

Leadership is a relationship between leaders and led. The leader interacts with individual followers but also critically with followers as collectives—social groups and teams. All that we know about group behavior thus becomes highly relevant to the challenges of leadership. Leaders need a set of concepts to understand the groups they must interact with. But this is not just a passive process of understanding as they act to change group balance in pursuit of their overarching purpose. They are, of course, rewriting the context.

Unleashing the Tiger Within

As with most human abilities, the talent for situation sensing comes partly from our genetic makeup, and is partly related to our socialization experiences and critical developmental moments in our life. Just as with golf, aspiring leaders could throw their hands in the air and say, "I'll never hit the ball like Tiger Woods." Or they can say, "OK, I may never hit it like Tiger—but I can sure get better."

The most important thing to recognize is that situation sensing can be taught and learned. Leading business schools have developed courses in "interpersonal skills training." Central to any improvement in this area is improved situation sensing. One technique is to videotape executives in specific situations—setting targets, giving feedback, communicating vision—and then review them working through what may have been missed or misinterpreted. Our experience of such courses highlights the common neglect of observational skills. Many driven executives will not give themselves the time to spend on simply watching what is going on around them. Their desire to get things done leads them to neglect even the simplest observational tasks. And of course, skilled observation is not easy. Think about how we experience a visit to an art gallery; if you can use the audio guide, you simply see more things. Leaders need that guide playing all the time.

Leaders, especially in large organizations, can develop networks that collect soft data for them. Many leaders in geographically dispersed organizations report that they nurture old connections—often way down the hierarchy—that keep them in touch with how things are feeling in layers of the organizations they would not otherwise easily reach. Cazzato and Bowmer both kept in touch with old sales colleagues, using informal occasions to elicit information unfiltered by hierarchies.

All of this goes to prove that situation sensing is not a passive process—leaders read and rewrite the context in order to achieve their overarching purpose.

The point those who aspire to leadership must arrive at is wonderfully captured in the following observation of politicians. "It has been said of two British Prime Ministers that one possessed no antennae, while the other possessed nothing else. If by antennae we understand alertness to nuance and undertone, it is easy to see how either tendency can lead to failure in business and government. The man who is all perception is likely to reflect the prevailing mood without adding direction of his own; the leader deaf to the moods and feelings of others may produce clear-cut plans but will be unable to gauge their acceptability."[13]

You can lead a team from anywhere so long as you know where you are. Think of golf's 2004 Ryder Cup, which brought together an American team with some of the best players in the world and a European team with some less-well-ranked players drawn from a number of countries. The key difference was that the Europeans were well led. The German captain, Bernhard Langer, displayed superb situation-sensing skills—at both the individual and team levels—while the hapless American captain, Hal Sutton, struck one false note after another. The Europeans won convincingly.[14]

FIVE

Remain Authentic— but Conform Enough

I N CHAPTER 4, we focused on the reading and rewriting task that leaders face with respect to both individuals and teams. But they must also read the organizational context. This involves understanding the complex social architecture to which the leader must adapt in order to obtain traction in the organization.[1]

The crucial word here is *adapt*. Leaders must conform *enough* if they are to make the connections necessary to deliver *change*. Leaders who succeed in changing organizations challenge the norms—but rarely all of them, all at once. They do not seek out instant head-on confrontation without understanding the organizational context. Indeed, survival (particularly in the early days) requires measured adaptation to an ongoing, established set of social relationships and organizational networks. To change an organization, the leader must first gain at least minimal acceptance as a member—and the rules for early survival are rarely the same as the rules for longer-term success.

Reading Organizations

Over the last two decades, there have been countless examples of CEOs who rode roughshod over organizational contexts. Sometimes they have reaped short-term gains. But in the long term, ignoring the organizational context is not an option. Sustainable change requires that the leader understand and tune in to the organizational context. Having done so, the leader can instigate change with credibility and with a greater chance of success. Ignore it and the results can be disastrous. Think of Al Dunlap, or the host of ruthless downsizers and asset strippers who conspicuously fail to deliver long-term change.

When Michael Ovitz joined Disney, for instance, he seemed to get this badly wrong. His colleague Michael Eisner claimed:

> He started to rub people the wrong way. He was controversial
> and it got worse as things went on . . . We'd all take a bus (at
> the corporate retreat) and he had a limousine; a special driver.
> Everyone had a walkie talkie and you heard walkie talkies
> around this 30,000 acres saying, "Who was this guy and why
> was he demanding this?" The perception was that Michael
> Ovitz was a little elitist for the egalitarian Walt Disney World
> in Florida. It was a bad vibe, let's put it that way.[2]

Ovitz lasted fourteen months.[3] In the 1990s, Robert Horton lasted just three years as chairman and CEO of the oil giant BP.

Horton's conspicuous display of his daunting intelligence some-times appeared arrogant and self-aggrandizing. In terms of corpo-rate strategy, Horton was clearly doing things the company badly needed, but he couldn't carry the troops along on the mission. His excessively autocratic style did not work in BP's polite culture. He didn't conform enough to persuade people to follow.

Durk Jager at P&G is another high-profile failure. Critics accused him of trying to change things "too much too fast." He lasted less than eighteen months. Warren Bennis has observed that Jager's suc-cessor, A. G. Lafley, "seemed at first to back off from Jager's com-mitment to 'stretch and speed,' but in fact Lafley has been able to bring about change every bit as radical as any Jager spoke of, including going outside the company for new ideas, a reversal of P&G's traditional 'invented here' philosophy. How did Lafley man-age? 'I didn't attack . . . I avoided saying P&G people are bad . . . I preserved the core of the culture and pulled people where I wanted to go. I enrolled them in change. I didn't tell them.'"[4]

Lafley's leadership illustrates the skill of reading the context and conforming enough—to achieve traction and deliver change.

But it's not just at the top that conforming enough matters. Our favorite bar in New York City appointed a new bar manager. He was irritated by the rather laid-back attitude of the staff, who ran tabs for too long for their regular customers. He thought the décor and the lighting too low. He tried to change it all at once. The customers deserted in droves, and before long the owner had to intervene and move him on.

The Full Monty

The question is, Who can read organizations well and how do they develop this skill? Clearly, some leaders are able to intuitively read situations largely on the back of many years' experience in different contexts. They develop a kind of wisdom that means that they are less dependent on conceptual models to give them insight or even to guide their interventions. But are there universal principles that underlie organizational relationships and that might frame possibilities for change? We think there are. Our consulting work suggests that many people find models that refine their context-reading skills.

We have developed a way of understanding organizational context that is based on a view of organizations as communities. In our model, drawing heavily on classic sociology, there are two key cultural relationships: *sociability* and *solidarity*.[5] Sociability refers primarily to affective relations between individuals who are likely to see each other as friends. They tend to share ideas and values and to associate with each other on equal terms. At its heart, sociability represents a relationship valued for its own sake. It is usually initiated through face-to-face contact, though it may be maintained through other forms of communication, and is characterized by high levels of mutual help. No real conditions are attached.

Solidarity, by contrast, describes task-focused cooperation between individuals and groups. It does not depend on close friendship or even personal acquaintance, nor does it need to be continuous. It arises only from a perception of shared interest—and when this occurs, solidarity can produce intense focus.

Although this discussion may seem a little abstract, relationships of sociability and solidarity are actually all around us—in our families, sports teams, social clubs, and communities. Arguably, this ubiquity is what drew the attention of the early sociologists in the first place. In effect, we all have an interest in—and are affected by—these relationships. Ask someone to describe their ideal family, for example, and typically they will tell you it is one where the members like and love one another (sociability) and one that pulls together when times get tough (solidarity).

Much popular fiction, drama, and film addresses one or both of these relationships. The movie *The Full Monty*, for example, develops a plot in which a group of low-morale, unemployed men move from negative, interpersonal rivalry to a crescendo of friendship and solidarity (between men *and* women) in the dramatic, striptease finale. Think too of the high levels of sociability and solidarity among the central characters of classic movies such as *Four Weddings and a Funeral, The Untouchables, Butch Cassidy and the Sundance Kid,* and even *The Godfather*.

Sociability Plus

For leaders in organizations, both sociability and solidarity confer certain advantages. But as we worked with these concepts in practice, we realized that each had both positive and negative dimensions. Take sociability. Its benefits are clear and substantial.

In high-sociability cultures, people enjoy their working lives, and we have known for a very long time that when people enjoy their work, they tend to be more productive.[6] Second, sociability helps in the process of innovation. Often, creativity is sparked by the sharing of half-formed ideas and is fostered by processes of debate and cross-fertilization—often in an unplanned way. This explains why we can talk of artistic or scientific movements; individuals come together to share in a friendly, supportive setting.

Finally, high-sociability workplaces are characterized by people working hard for each other. You hear these kinds of conversations: "Sorry, I'll be home late tonight—I'm helping Bill finish a presentation for tomorrow." We have become more and more convinced of the benefits of sociability at work—especially when innovation is a business imperative.

However, it has become equally clear that there is a downside to sociability at work. We may be inclined to indulge the inadequate performance of others who we regard as friends. And of course, the more we come to know people, the more likely we are to see them as friends. As George Homans insightfully remarked, "You can get to like some queer old people if you spend enough time with them."[7]

Sociability can lead to indulgence and compromise. But perhaps even more insidious is the process of clique formation. Cliques inhibit change and stifle the attempts of leaders to galvanize the organization. People in one financial services company we worked with often told us that the place was controlled by a shadowy clique called "the brotherhood." "How will we know who they are?" we asked. "You'll know when you cross them!" we were warned. Whether the clique existed or not is beside the point. People believed it existed, and that said a great deal about the organization's culture.

Similar processes of clique formation have inhibited the growth prospects of high-tech firms attempting to move beyond the vision of the founder and the close coterie of originals. High-sociability cultures, in both their positive and their negative forms, generate significant challenges for leaders.

Solidarity

Similarly, solidarity confers considerable advantages in an organizational culture, but its negative aspects present enormous challenges to leaders. The first benefit is a tremendous degree of focus. In addition, this focus on clear measurable objectives can be mobilized swiftly. In high-solidarity cultures, a common perception of shared interests produces rapid, targeted actions. This ability to deploy organizational capability in such a timely fashion is, of course, a huge benefit. Indeed, strategic thinkers used to advocate this model as the very essence of a successful business enterprise.[8]

Yet even solidarity has negative aspects. The first of these is paradoxical but can be highly damaging. The problem is this: organizations displaying some of the negative aspects of solidarity can do the wrong things highly efficiently. They march over the cliff in perfect step. To use a 1990s mantra, organizational members are required to "just do it" rather than contemplating any wider ramifications. Such organizations are intolerant of dissent. You must either fit in or leave. The leader may find him- or herself surrounded by unquestioning agreement—a poor indicator of organizational health. This very emphasis on conformity makes leadership difficult.

In addition, solidarity predisposes organizations to high degrees of instrumentalism. When asked to kick around some half-formed thoughts, colleagues are likely to say that they are too busy to help; worse still, they may ask, "What's in it for me?" Worse still, perhaps, they may think, but not say, "Why should I help you? We're rivals." Finally, in its negative form, solidarity may coalesce around functional or divisional interests so that individuals see the world through the eyes of marketing, finance, production, or R&D, rather than taking an overall view of the organization's best interests. Turf battles are a likely outcome as factions begin to appear. Again, the leadership challenges of mitigating the negative form of high solidarity are considerable.

We ran the two concepts against each other to produce the Double S Cube, shown in figure 5-1.[9]

Quadrophenic Cultures

We distinguish four fundamental types of organizational culture, each of which has both a positive and a negative face. *Networked cultures* exhibit high levels of sociability but relatively low

FIGURE 5-1

Double S cube

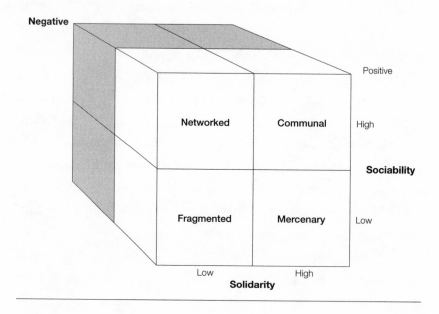

levels of solidarity. They are often characterized by a friendly, fam-
ily-like ethos. There are significant work-related social events, and
these act to preserve and extend friendship patterns. Sociability
often extends outside the workplace via social and sporting clubs
that frequently involve whole families.

Networked cultures exhibit a number of negative manifestations.
These include clique formation; informal information exchanges
that can degenerate into dangerous rumor and gossip machines;
friendly meetings that produce lots of talk but little action; and,
most significantly, considerable energy, especially among senior
managers, that goes into organizational politics and making the
right impression. There is often more emphasis on managing up-
ward than managing outcomes.

In stark contrast are *mercenary cultures*, which display high solidarity and low sociability. In organizations with this kind of culture, there is often a heightened sense of competition and a strong desire to win. Winning is thought of as a zero-sum game: "I win—you lose." Shared values are built around competitive individualism and clear personal achievement goals. Cooperative activity occurs only where there are clear measurable benefits. Effective teamwork was once described to us in an archetypal mercenary organization as "eagles flying in formation."

Such cultures produce formidable business enterprises, but, again, there are negatives to consider. The focus on the clearly measurable means that important, but tough-to-measure, issues are missed. Internal competition can become widespread. Perhaps most damaging of all in knowledge-based businesses, there is a low level of emotional involvement with the organization, leading to a brittle psychological contract, with associated risks of losing key players.

Fragmented cultures—low on sociability and solidarity—are unusual but in some contexts can survive and flourish. For example, businesses that rely on outsourcing, home-based work, or individual expertise may be predominantly fragmented. The freedom given to individuals in these cultures can generate substantial benefits. Think of the autonomy of a university professor or a senior partner in a law firm and the creativity this can generate. But if the freedoms are abused, fragmented cultures can be characterized by selfish and secretive behavior. Even simple attempts to cooperate—meetings, for example—can be undermined by too many individuals driven by their own personal agendas.

Finally, *communal cultures* are high on both sociability and solidarity. On the face of it, these have the best of both worlds. Their appeal has certainly been celebrated in accounts of innovative high-performance businesses—think of Apple, Microsoft, or Ben and Jerry's. These are companies that are passionate about a cause, with members working together in a tightly knit team atmosphere. When companies like these are at their best, the alignment between espoused values and real practices can be extraordinary.

But they can also become vulnerable to the paradox of success. In effect, they begin to believe that they are invulnerable. Competitors or customers may be too easily dismissed as "wrong," and values or principles sustained beyond their useful purpose. In the 1980s and early 1990s, IBM suffered some of the downsides of a negative communal culture. Ironically, Apple, the new entrant that helped undermine IBM's position, went on to also suffer from a similar complacency.

Freeze, Please, Tease

Leaders act within these basic organizational culture models. Indeed, within individual organizations, there will always be significant subcultural variations. Think, for example, of the difference between a communal R&D team and the typically mercenary sales force that must sell the product they develop. While effective leaders are adept at revealing appropriate aspects of their authentic personalities at the right time, they are also adept at tuning in to the individual, team, and organizational context.

The question must be why they bother to tune in to the context if leadership is about being true to yourself? The answer is that leaders who succeed in being their authentic selves do so with a significant caveat: paradoxically, they accept some degree of conformity. They are authentic and make use of their intrinsic differences, but they also conform *enough* to get things done within the constraints of the organizational culture.

The leaders we studied were able to read the organizational culture and conform enough to be accepted as an insider. Most importantly, they did so without compromising their authenticity. They adapted their authentic selves to the organizational context in a way that engaged with and, where necessary, showed respect for (or at least tolerance of) the existing culture. This delicate balancing act has been familiar for decades to many female executives in male-dominated managerial hierarchies. Early and open confrontation of certain (unacceptable) male norms may sometimes be necessary. Equally, however, some women are able to take on negative female stereotypes (nurturer, seductress, secretary, iron maiden, and so on) and turn them to their advantage. This is impossible without maintaining a healthy sense of role distance and a firm eye on the ultimate goal. But by conforming enough, some women are able to survive, then connect to gain traction, and ultimately deliver longer-term change.

A historical parallel here would be Alexander the Great, who famously adopted many of the traditions of the peoples he conquered. This meant he was more easily accepted as the ruler. Similarly, local rulers in the Roman Empire were known for their tolerance toward the local customs of their occupied territories.[10]

In the modern organizational sense, failure to make the necessary adjustment can result in the culture rejecting the leader—or more likely, failing to engage with them. At the same time, there is a danger of conforming too much. This can result in the leader losing their authenticity—the equivalent of going native. So how do effective leaders pull off this balancing act?

People who retain their authenticity in a leadership position are able to show who they are—through self-disclosure—because they know where they come from. They are rooted. They have an understanding of what made them. But this, in itself, is not enough. During the course of our lives, we face new situations—often a long way from our origins. Effective leaders handle these new situations well. They are comfortable not only with their origins, but also with the movement that life brings.

We are all, of course, interested in people's origins. We know that it helps us to understand people better. Knowing the factors that shaped individuals gives us a better handle on relating to them now. For many years, we have worked with a wise senior executive of a U.S. chemical company. He begins his conversations with new members of his team with this request: "Tell me how you came to be the kind of guy you are now." He has an almost insatiable interest in the complex sets of factors that explain who we are.

Our understanding of this process arose originally by observing the effects of social mobility on executives, mainly males. Both through our work in business schools and in our consultancy and through direct work in organizations, we developed a model to explain individuals' experiences of social mobility through their organizational lives and their differential responses to it. We call it the *freeze-please-tease* model.

Some individuals are so in awe of their destination that they freeze—losing the very leadership attributes that took them there in the first place. Others attempt, inauthentically, to ape the cultural mores of their new social context: they please. These, too, lose their leadership capability. The most effective groups are those who retain their authenticity but make some cultural adjustments to their new social milieu. In other words, they tease, retaining their authenticity, but acquiring enough of the behaviors of their new situation to be able to operate effectively—and critically—to achieve their purpose.

The key concept that underlies this model is the notion of cultural capital. This idea comes from the work of the French sociologist Pierre Bourdieu.[11] He argues that just as social groups in society have differential access to material resources, so access to the most desired cultural forms is rationed. Thus, in art, literature, education, fashion, and food, dominant social groups are able to make their definition of culture the most desired. They may even use this to screen out others, who lack this cultural capital.

This is a complex argument, but we have seen it play out many times. As individuals move through organizations, they are exposed to dominant forms of cultural capital. Some handle it, and some do not. The following examples are, of necessity, anonymous, but they are based on firsthand observation.

Frozen Development

Bill was an excellent electrical engineer. He had started as a trainee electrician, and his abilities had been swiftly spotted by the large utility company in Pennsylvania where he worked. The HR department at his company persuaded him (and it took some persuasion) to go to university, where the company sponsored him to study electrical engineering. Initially, he found university hard. He was mixing with people from backgrounds very different from his, including many students from other countries. However, he worked hard, and his brightness soon captured the attention of his teachers. This gave him legitimacy with his peers, especially as he was always willing to help those less able than himself.

Bill graduated with a good degree and was warmly welcomed back to work. By now he had married his childhood sweetheart and was enjoying life. We first encountered him when he was identified by his company as a high-potential young executive. We both worked with him and could see his potential. He worked hard on developing his strategic capabilities and using his good, rather direct interpersonal skills, and moved swiftly through the organization. His work often involved project management skills, and he became adept at assembling and leading teams. His technical ability and straightforward honesty were his biggest leadership attributes.

Things started to go wrong when he was moved to the head office, an advisory role to some of the most senior executives in the company. HR had rightly seen this as good preparation for a major leadership position back in the line. But the head office was political. Bill found that his straight-talking style hit many wrong notes. He started to get feedback that he didn't fully understand the complexity of situations, that he should widen his range of influencing skills. He began to seriously doubt his own abilities. Bill tried to curb his directness, but he could never mimic the political behavior of his superiors. He started to lose his way.

We saw him again back in the line—now in a significant leadership role. We had expected him to do well, but Bill's sense of himself had been knocked. He was increasingly plagued by self-doubt. Perhaps he should have stuck to just being a good engineer; maybe this leadership stuff just was not for him. His behavior increasingly swung between indecisive, while he tried to read the politics, and sudden bursts of outright aggression as he struggled to find his old forthrightness.

He is still there, but probably will not progress further. He has lost the capacity to be himself with skill; he is effectively frozen. He found himself in a social milieu where he could not be himself.

Anxious to Please

Contrast Bill's case with Graham's. We first met him as a highly energetic sales guy in a fast-moving consumer goods business in Boston. He was, and is, a very effective salesman, albeit in a rather old-fashioned, in-your-face way. Some people found him rather brash. We always related well to him as he shares our passion for sports, best discussed over a glass of decent beer. He was delighted at the resurgence of microbreweries and took pleasure in sharing with us his latest find. He was clearly very bright but a little too energetic and forthright for the rather politely sociable culture in which he worked. We urged people to give him a chance to grow, feeling that his high-energy leadership style was just what was required, at least in some parts of his organization.

Graham moved from sales to marketing, then briefly into a production role at a factory, and then back into a senior marketing role. We were amazed at the transformation. Rather than threatening the cozy sociability of the organizational culture, he seemed to exemplify it. His speech had become nuanced and his opinions carefully measured. We found him defending the status quo, observing that our insistence on a change agenda for the organization was just a little simplistic. He even expressed the view that he rather preferred the quiet corridors of the head office to the hurly-burly of the marketplace. Was this the same man, we asked ourselves? He had certainly changed; we tried talking baseball, but his sporting passions were now sailing and skiing in the Rockies.

Of course, interpreting these changes is not simple. One view is that Graham had simply matured, that his new functional experiences and exposure to the corporate center had deepened his understanding of the issues his organization faced. Our view is different. In his attempts to fit in to the dominant corporate culture, he had lost just what made him so useful as a change leader in the organization. In his attempt to please, he had lost those individual differences that he had previously used so effectively in a leadership role.

These two examples—one of *freeze*, the other of *please*—show talented executives losing some of their directness as they move up the organization. But the process is not always like this.

Kevin works for a large brewing company—in fact, one of the largest in the world. He is a scientist, and his obsession is yeast, a very important substance to a brewing company. He is rather shy, an introvert who relates best to other scientists, though there are few who can match his knowledge of yeasts, or indeed his interest in them. All of those who work with him testify to his intellectual capability, his deep loyalty to the company, and his passion for their products. His almost naïve enthusiasm for his subject was a considerable leadership asset—among the research community at least.

Kevin's success with using yeasts for new product development brought him wider attention in the organization. He moved to a much more senior role in product development. Here his peers were largely from the marketing function. In the brewing business, this function is often dominated by boisterous extroverts whose interests usually encompass sports and the consumption of their products.

In this new environment, Kevin was a fish out of water. He became lonely and more introverted. His performance tailed off. To have a significant impact on the new-product development process, he needed to get close to those who knew the market research function and controlled marketing spending. This was a milieu he simply could not operate in. Kevin came to hate the ebullient behavior of his colleagues. In turn, they saw him as a rather boring obsessive. Since Kevin was unable to acquire sufficient social capital to engage with his colleagues, his career is now stalled, and he is looking to leave the company.

Teasing out Authenticity

Our last example is much more positive. It tells the story of a former student of ours. She was bright and hard working and well liked by both her peers and the faculty who taught her. Sarah comes from a region in the United Kingdom with a distinctive but rather unfashionable accent. Some of our colleagues felt that in the fevered labor market for MBAs from top schools, she would suffer as a result. In any event, she decided not to pursue a career in either consulting or investment banking, the favored route for many of her high-flying colleagues. Rather, she took a job in a well-respected fast-moving consumer goods (FMCG) company, where she made good progress in the marketing function.

All seemed to be going well, but the travel demands of an increasingly international job began to take their toll. Rather reluctantly, she decided to move to one of the most blue-chip of executive search firms. We kept in touch and saw how her leadership ability was growing. Sarah took every opportunity to extend her skills, and we watched (it has to be said with some pride) as it became clear that she had every chance of running one of the major parts of the organization. There were subtle changes in her demeanor. She had always possessed a certain calm intensity—but she added a sense of gravitas that was serious but never pompous.

She moved easily into a world of main board directors, and several CEOs regarded her as a trusted adviser. Sarah clearly works hard to make herself valuable and acceptable in this world. But she has never lost that sense of who she really is. Her accent is still there, softened a little from much travel, but distinctive nonetheless. She is as happy in a downtown bar as she is in a swanky hotel lounge. Indeed, she often takes people to surprising locations, especially when she is collecting information. It is clear that both among her staff and in the marketplace, she is viewed as a real person, with a life outside of work. At the same time, she has conformed enough to the rather rarefied social milieu in which she has to operate. Like all effective leaders, she has conformed enough to ensure traction and the achievement of her purpose. But she has also retained a kind of playfulness about her role. It is really her, but it is as if she is watching herself and smiling at her success. Those she leads will sometimes insightfully remark that despite her remarkable openness, Sarah remains just a little enigmatic.

Conforming Enough

Sarah exemplifies the "tease" approach to conforming enough. She has realized that being authentic is not enough for leadership. Effective leaders both challenge *and* conform. They practice deeply held principles *but* also compromise. They give of themselves *but* still practice a degree of role distance. They are resolutely nonhierarchical but are adept at using hierarchies.

Consider Niall FitzGerald, former joint chair of the huge foods and detergents company Unilever. FitzGerald understands the behaviors needed to operate in a complex, highly *networked* international culture. He has excellent interpersonal skills, with an Irish twinkle, and can be extremely charming. He learned that Unilever's is not a culture where an abrasive leadership style plays well, so he can schmooze with the best, sharing and collecting personal information while chatting about business issues. Over the years, he cultivated a complex social network throughout this global giant. It enabled him to get things done within the Unilever culture, often outside formal systems.

FitzGerald seemed to have adapted to this networked culture perfectly. But don't be fooled. Together with colleague Anthony Bergmans, FitzGerald produced much radical change. This included pruning the brand portfolio, focusing on growth, acquiring Best

Foods, and in general bringing a much clearer performance focus. This was a difficult process, and the outcome remains unclear. But whatever the final verdict, none of this would have been achieved without careful use of his knowledge of the culture—in both its positive and negative manifestations.

Just as he built a network of social relationships that enable him to get things done, FitzGerald also identified those negative networks that inhibit the successful implementation of change. He knows the silent enemies as well as the enthusiastic followers. He is more than capable of "flushing out the traitors." As a result, he both maintained the integrity of his vision for Unilever and adapted to the critical requirements of the culture. FitzGerald remained his own man, with an intense and compelling view of Unilever's future, but recognized the significance of the organization's complex social fabric for anyone seeking to exercise a leadership role in this culture.

The Essential Leader

Similarly global in his ability to sense a networked organization context is Bill Burns. He is acutely aware of the need for cultural adjustment as he moves between Roche's operations in Europe, the United States, and Japan. As he freely admits, he needs to act differently in the Genentech business in California than in the Chugai partnership in Japan. But despite these switches in behavior, he is always concerned to act within what he calls "a recognizable bandwidth," to communicate, in effect, an essential Bill. Talk to his colleagues, and all are quick to applaud his personal warmth, consideration, and decency—as well as his sharp eye for the detail of product performance.

Operating in a very different organizational context is Belmiro de Azevedo, president of Portugal's largest company, the veneers to telecoms multinational Sonae. Belmiro absolutely exemplifies the company's lead-or-out meritocratic culture.

Now in his early sixties, Belmiro still plays squash and soccer and works out regularly at the company gym. He understands exactly how to behave in this culture: know your numbers, never express opinions without a deep understanding of the underlying measures, be able to make tough decisions—about business and people. All of this makes him sound hard and distant, but that is to misunderstand his leadership style and his own strong sense of individuality and authenticity. This is best expressed in the annual trip he and his friends make to his origins in the beautiful Douro Valley of northern Portugal. This is a celebration of where he comes from—what has made him who he is. It involves a visit to the countryside where his parents lived, some delicious local food, traditional dancing—all in a spirit of friendship and fun. It is profoundly humanizing. Belmiro knows how to succeed at Sonae, but he has never lost sight of his own origins or his humanity.

While in her role as HR director of the retailer Marks & Spencer, Jean Tomlin aimed to remain herself in the context of a long-standing, close, and rather traditional *communal* culture. This is a culture that historically demanded high levels of conformity at both the behavioral and the values level. The challenge for her was to exemplify and practice core organizational values while retaining a commitment to changing in response to fierce competition. This meant that in public she acknowledged key values and current lines of activity.

Jean told us that in any new job, she plans on showing her people just 50 percent of herself in the first three months—and showing even that very gradually. In one-on-one interactions, her aim was to initiate what she calls "authentic conversations" designed to "puncture the veneer." In these encounters, she saw the enemies as complacency and "disciple-ism"—the unquestioning following of leaders. This encapsulates the leadership challenges to be found in such cultures. On one hand, the challenge is to be a passionate advocate of key organizational values, and on the other, to maintain a degree of critical distance. This balancing act was accentuated for Jean Tomlin as a black British woman. Jean helped the company through a fraught period of change, and the process continues. But arguably, producing change in a long-established communal culture is the most difficult challenge of all. With Marks & Spencer facing continuing pressure from shareholders and possible predators, Jean has moved on. The context around her has changed yet again, and, as we have repeatedly stressed, leadership will always expose individuals to personal risk.

Uniquely You

These issues aren't the sole preserve of conservative organizations or labyrinthine multinationals. The same kind of leadership challenges might be found at other communal culture companies, such as Apple, Hewlett-Packard, and Johnson & Johnson, or at smaller, highly creative companies like the computer games developer Electronic Arts Inc. (EA).

At EA in Europe, for example, the challenge for David Gardner's successor, Gerhard Florin, is to engage with his colleagues in a way that sustains the company's strong people values while simultaneously consolidating the company's commercial values in a fiercely competitive, fast-changing market. As a German, ex-McKinsey consultant, Florin cuts a very different figure from the Californian, EA-lifer Gardner. Clearly, Gerhard is not David—and he must use his unique strengths to advantage to carry the company forward. But at the same time, he must be careful to honor EA's strong cultural values of teamwork, creativity, and individual freedom. He knows that without this, he is unlikely to gain the traction necessary for change.

In professional services firms, where the dominant culture is often individualized and *fragmented*, the leadership challenges are different again. Take the case of Ian Powell, U.K. leader of PricewaterhouseCoopers Business Recovery Services practice. This highly successful business with global market leadership has forty-five partners in the United Kingdom. All of them have made it either through their leading-edge technical knowledge or their deal-making, entrepreneurial skills. For the best, it's a combination of both.

Powell would very much like to change the culture—building strong interpersonal connections and a clear performance focus so that the business can exploit cross-selling opportunities, share knowledge, and increase levels of innovation. In order to do this, he has begun a series of organizational development initiatives. But first he has to establish his own leadership credentials.

In such a context, this requires demonstrating to his partners that he can personally win and deliver "big cases." For example, he was the administrator of the Rover/MG Group following the collapse of the deal with the Shanghai Automobile Company. He must show that his contacts, both internally and especially externally, are very valuable to the business. Even as he begins to change the culture, he continues to reinforce his legitimacy as a "good hunter." In addition, he exemplifies the new behaviors that he wishes to become embedded in the culture. He coaches, mentors, builds teams—he is informal and rather nonhierarchical—much more like his real self, if you like, but he never loses sight of the necessity to conform enough to the particular culture of a high-performing professional services firm.

Just like professional service firms, museums are often dominated by highly individualistic experts: curators, scientists, and researchers. As a result, their cultures can be *fragmented* and dominated by rather private and, at their worst, selfish behavior. As newly appointed deputy director of the British Museum, Dawn Austwick was shocked by some of what she found on her arrival. "People were used to being ignored. They would walk past you and not look at you. The new director [Neil McGregor] and I made a point of beaming a 'hello' or 'good morning' to everyone. It was a shock to them!"

With a £6 million deficit, Dawn and Neil McGregor had to confront several norms early—not just the social pleasantries. But she was careful not to try to change things too fast. "The museum is steeped in ritual and tradition. The trustees have met on a Saturday once a month for the past 250 years. At the center of the table is the mace . . . alongside such symbols there are important values of expertise and quality which are interwoven into the fabric. Some consultants would tend to come in and say, 'Sort it out'—but you cannot wade in and expect to fix everything swiftly. You cannot issue edicts. You need to know which battles to fight, when to be discreet and when to bide your time."

In her previous role, Dawn was the project manager for the creation of the Tate Modern, one of the great public-sector success stories of contemporary Britain. This £130 million project started from a blank page. But as Dawn has recognized, by contrast, the British Museum has a long-established culture that must, at least in part, be respected if successful change and development are to eventually be delivered. The museum's cost base has now been reduced by £6.5 million, and in 2003–2004 it reported an operating surplus of £1.7 million. Dawn and her colleagues are now focusing on the next steps.

Traction Men and Women

All of these examples show leaders with the determination to change their situation, but also with an ability to gain enough organizational leverage by adjusting enough to the critical aspects of their cultural context. They retain and express their authentic selves but conform enough. As Warren Bennis remarked:

> Your first acts will win people over or they will turn people against you, sometimes permanently. And those initial acts may have a long lasting effect on how the group performs. It is, therefore, almost always best for the novice to make a low key entry. This buys you time to gather information and to develop relationships wisely. It gives you an opportunity to learn the culture of the organization and to benefit from the wisdom of those who are already there . . . it shows them that you are a leader, not a dictator.[12]

Authenticity in a leadership role means more than just being yourself. It must also involve consistency and coherence within and between the leader's various roles. Critically, it entails a sense of comfort both with origins, that which makes us what we are, and destinations, the places that life experiences take us to. You can describe it as authenticity involving consciousness (self-knowledge/ awareness), coherence (self-consistency), and comfort (what could be called *self-groundedness*). But authenticity on its own is not enough.

Perhaps the best example we have ever seen involved one of the first female finance directors in a Japanese company. She was Japanese but had extensive experience in the U.S. pharmaceutical business. She was a marvelous change leader—modernizing accounting practices, bringing in new talent, disturbing some cozy high-sociability relationships among the senior men of the company—but she always appropriately played the role of a Japanese woman in social settings. Everyone understood that she could be very tough, but she conformed enough to the prevailing social norms in order to achieve her objectives. Hers was a leadership performance of great subtlety and skill.

In order for leaders to make a real impact on their organizations, they must achieve this sort of "traction." They must engage with organizational life in a way that creates the possibility of making change happen. So, to the three ingredients of authenticity—consciousness, coherence, and consistency—we would add a fourth for those who want to make a real difference: a necessary degree of clever conformity.

SIX

Manage Social Distance

EFFECTIVE LEADERS ARE ABLE to evoke high levels of emotional response, loyalty, and affection. They can empathize with those they lead, step into their shoes, get close to them. Yet they also seem able to communicate a sense of edge, to remind people of the job at hand and the overarching purpose of the collective endeavor. In doing so, they move skillfully from closeness to distance and back again. They are able to get close to their followers yet, paradoxically, keep their distance.[1]

Rick Dobbis is well known in the music industry for the loyalty—even love—he inspires. Dobbis seldom loses any executive he wants to keep. His people prize the close relationships they have with him, along with his praise for their good work—praise that is hard earned and all the more valuable for that. So it came as a bit of a shock to two of his staffers attending a global marketing meeting in London when Dobbis gave them an intense public grilling on their failure to produce a marketing plan on time. They got a bigger shock at the evening's elegant cocktail party. When Dobbis saw the two men talking, he marched over and caustically asked if they had finished the plan yet. They were taken aback. They had assumed it was a time for relaxation, but left the party and uncomplainingly went back to the office.

Tough Love

One of the authors got a personal taste of the Dobbis treatment when he worked with him, and sometimes for him, at PolyGram Music in the 1990s. Rick once asked Gareth to prepare a series of service contracts for companies in eastern Europe. Gareth knew he was running late on the job. So when Rick sent word for Gareth to come to his office, it was clear there was going to be trouble. Sure enough, there were none of his usual pleasantries, just "Are the contracts done yet?" The result was that Gareth went straight back to work, and the contracts were finished by lunchtime that day. The treatment worked. And Gareth didn't resent it. Rick is an excellent manager and, when Gareth isn't working for him, a good friend.

Dobbis himself tends to think of his role-switching trait almost as a character flaw. "I know that there's a part of me that has a tendency to flip from very positive to very negative very quickly," he told us. Once, someone even suggested that he needed medication for bipolar disorder. Still, he argues, as long as his relationships are built around trust, respect, and personal warmth, his people can handle "the moments when it gets a little ugly. If it's a good relationship, I can deal with it in context and not feel that the relationship has been ruined. But I'm aware that I have a problem with being theatrical."

In reality, Rick Dobbis's "problem" is an indispensable skill of authentic leadership.

Inventing Distance

The concept of social distance derives originally from the German-born sociologist Georg Simmel. Writing in the early twentieth century, Simmel conceived of social distance as a complex interpretation of sociability, as forms of distance in both a geometric and a metaphoric sense.[2] In modern social science, it has increasingly been seen as a measure of intimacy between groups and individuals. In turn, the degree of intimacy directly affects the degree of influence that one individual may have over another.

There are good reasons for believing that the skillful management of social distance is becoming even more important for leaders. Hierarchies, for example, are becoming flatter, partly for cost control reasons but mainly to increase speed of response to customer desires and market changes. Hierarchies have always been much more than structural devices. They have also been sources of meaning for people.[3] Moving through stable hierarchies gave the illusion of becoming more of a leader. Indeed, the "lazy" senior executive relied on the crutch of hierarchy to establish social distance, jealously guarding their status privileges as a way of establishing their difference.[4]

Those days are gone. Leaders now need distance to establish perspective, to see the big things that may shape the future of the organization, and closeness, to know what is really going on inside their business; and they cannot rely on hierarchy to supply the former.

This movement between closeness and distance is rather like a dance, with leaders basing their movement and timing on refined situation-sensing skills. It is just one of the adjustments they must constantly make and remake at the core of the leadership relationship. The balance for any leader is forever changing. This explains why style theory was unable to identify the one best leadership style.

It is also worth noting that just as national cultures vary along the social distance scale, so, too, do organizational cultures. Leading with a predisposition to distance in the high-sociability cultures of Heineken, Unilever, or PWC is difficult. Equally, overemphasizing personal closeness and warmth at the expense of task achievement can be hazardous in high-solidarity cultures such as Mars or Procter & Gamble.

Friendship and Leadership

There is another major strand of social science—exemplified by the work of George Homans—that is also relevant.[5] This shows that humans find it easier to be close with those with whom they perceive similarities. It is easier to be close to people you like.

Leaders, of course, are not necessarily dealing with people they like. They must be able to manage social distance with a diverse range of people in a variety of contexts. Leadership, which always implies some overarching or coordinating purpose, is not a friendship contest. Leadership resembles friendship only because leaders must jettison or conceal some of their differences in order to establish a base for relationships and team building. But after that, it is the higher cause that gives the leader the authority needed to be close and still establish distance.

"Closeness" is likely to be expressed in a number of ways— varying always according to context. In some cases, the gap may not be large. Think, for example, of skilled male professionals with similar backgrounds working together in a small, low-hierarchy advertising agency. The scope for potential leaders to establish shared professional interests and personal empathy is likely to be high. The typical challenge for leaders in this environment is to establish distance.

In other contexts, the challenge may be the reverse. Consider an American woman establishing a retail chain in Japan. In this case, at least initially, there is likely to be ample scope for social distance. The greater challenge is likely to be in forging a sense of closeness. Where social differences are large, a sense of identification is often best achieved through the clarification of shared goals and interests. Establishing more "sociable" forms of closeness is likely to be more difficult, and perhaps culturally inappropriate.

There is one final fascinating complication here. While the concept of social distance applies universally to human relationships, the *manifestation* of closeness and distance varies between cultures. What closeness looks like or feels like in Tokyo will be different in London, New York, or Bangalore. This is another factor making leadership in an international context an even greater challenge.

Close But Not Too Close

A sense of closeness delivers two important benefits. First, it enables the leader to know and understand their followers—a vital prerequisite for effective leadership. Second, closeness enables the followers to know more of the leader. By being close, we show who we are. It offers a context for disclosure—of weakness as well as strength.

Our observations suggest that effective leaders take this opportunity for disclosure but remain in other ways interestingly

enigmatic. They disclose personal differences and human fallibility—but never entirely. In this context, the popularity of emotional
intelligence is worrying. The important point to realize is that being
intelligent with our emotions may require them to be hidden.
Sometimes good leadership involves *withholding* rather than displaying emotions, and maintaining distance.

Distance confers different advantages. Primary here is that distance signals to the followers that the leader has an overarching
purpose. Leadership is not an end in itself. Think back to Sir Richard
Sykes talking about a strand of DNA, or John Latham's belief in creating a positive educational environment for all his pupils. Remember also Marcia, the Puerto Rican American cleaning supervisor we
introduced in chapter 1, and her passion for clean offices. Her followers always knew where she stood and what they were there for.

To be legitimate, a leader always has a larger, superordinate
purpose. Establishing distance enables the leader to build solidarity
with followers based on a shared view of this overarching goal. When
great leaders do this skillfully, they do it in pursuit of a goal: making
money, building beautiful buildings, eradicating human illness, making great movies.

Some Are More Distant Than Others

All leaders possess an inbuilt, maybe hardwired, preference for
either closeness or distance.

The French leader Charles de Gaulle exemplified distance. De
Gaulle believed that a leader can have no authority without prestige,
nor prestige unless he keeps his distance. Former U.S. president
Richard Nixon wrote of him, "Whenever I met de Gaulle, whether
publicly or privately, he displayed an enormous, even stately, dig-
nity. His resolute bearing gave him an air of aloofness . . . He had a

certain ease of manner when dealing with another head of state, whom he considered an equal, but he was never informal, even with his closest friends."[6]

To maintain his mystique, de Gaulle avoided friendship with his colleagues. The most informal address he allowed was Mon Général. He is said to have transferred his personal staff after a certain period to avoid familiarity. He was polite at diplomatic functions, but kept his emotional warmth for the privacy of his family.

De Gaulle's leadership philosophy echoes the Persian tradition of establishing proper distance between the leader and the led. In his book *The Edge of the Sword*, de Gaulle wrote about the need for the leader to create and maintain mystique. "First and foremost, there can be no prestige without mystery, for familiarity breeds contempt. All religions have their tabernacles, and no man is a hero to his valet. In the designs, the demeanor, and the mental operations of a leader there must always be 'something' which others cannot altogether fathom, which puzzles them, stirs them, and rivets their attention . . . Aloofness, character and the personification of quietness, these qualities it is that surround with prestige those who are prepared to carry a burden that is too heavy for lesser mortals."[7]

Mind the Gap

John Birt, Greg Dyke's predecessor as director general of the BBC, also had a predisposition to distance. This gave him the perspective to recognize that the competitive terrain for broadcasting was changing. But he also found closeness difficult. He quickly lost touch with the BBC's own creative talent and became increasingly reliant on external advisors. Birt was widely seen as aloof, unable to communicate with people about their work. On dutiful visits to

BBC operations, Birt dressed in an Armani suit and spoke only to the department head.

When Birt announced a radical reorganization of the BBC, it came as a complete surprise to everyone in the organization except the board of directors, the McKinsey advisers who created the plan, and the personnel director who handled the McKinsey budget. There was an internal rebellion against the plan, but outsiders generally agreed that the reorganization would help prepare the BBC for a changing world.

Birt's default mode toward distance made it hard for him to connect with a wider cadre of managers and creatives at the BBC. He could not find a milieu in which to practice disclosure—to make his real leadership assets work beyond the small group with whom he had established, often rather painfully, social closeness.

What makes this case of wider significance is that introverts are overrepresented at the top of organizations, and many of them find establishing closeness difficult.[8] Introverts need time to establish closeness and reveal difference—and time is in short supply. The trouble is that much that has been written about leadership behavior plays to the predispositions of the extrovert. We need a "Leadership Guide for the Introvert."

Emotionally Abrupt

Sadly, there are all too many examples of leaders who overdo their social distance. We observed a research team leader at a pharmaceutical company based in the Research Triangle Park, in North Carolina. She is universally regarded as a brilliant young researcher, an energetic leader, and a genuinely nice person. She has a real talent for warmth and closeness, but in one-on-one sessions with her colleagues, she switches abruptly. She can be brutally candid, and this can be hurtful and damaging, especially to her elders. She hasn't grasped the concept of bandwidth—the principle that a leader must operate within recognized, accepted boundaries of variation. Her switches to distance are so extreme that they call into question whether her more agreeable traits are really authentic.[9]

Other leaders simply dismiss closeness. They seem to hang up their emotions when they enter the office, just as workers in the age of Taylorism were advised to hang up their brains. We worked with a manager at a luxury retailer in New York City. She was a genuine and warm Italian American. But she had made it to the top with a ruthless focus on results and beating the competition. Her people saw her as remote, unforgiving, tough to work for, and a bit of a brute. We showed her some 360-degree feedback from colleagues and suggested that it would be a big asset for her if she could show more of her emotional side at work. "I reserve that for home," she said. As a leader, that decision cost her dearly.

Her case illustrates why the concept of emotional intelligence has resonated for executives. Paraphrasing Daniel Goleman, effective leaders use their emotions to liberate the energy of others.[10] Of course, to "use" your emotions, you have first to know them. Many who make their way up organizational hierarchies have been positively discouraged from exploring their emotional life. Sometimes the damage is so deep that they have little chance of emotional reconnection. No surprise then that there is an epidemic of stress-related illness at work.[11]

Time for Distance

In general, leaders signal distance by managing the context of the meeting. Their language and bearing are formal rather than relaxed; they establish that the space is theirs; they use as many signals as they can to stress their authority, and they make sure the signals are consistent.

At a communication level, this may mean keeping messages short, direct, and authoritative: avoiding conditional forms of verbs (*could*, *should*, and *might*) and using active sentences and personal pronouns. It might also involve using silence and editing out the conversational preliminaries designed to ease social occasions.[12]

There are a host of other heavy-handed, but effective, ways of establishing distance. The *Dilbert* cartoon is filled with examples of executives with permanently closed doors, overprotective assistants, private dining rooms, executive lavatories, parking spaces by the front door, and so on.

While these are open to justifiable parody, at times distance is necessary. When Rick Dobbis confronted the two dilatory executives, it was a cold shock made all the more startling—and effective—by the warmth of the social occasion. Distance underscored the message. When leaders are dealing with issues of management performance, distance is useful, and often essential.

Sometimes a whole organization needs to confront its problems, and in such cases, a leader must use the distance treatment on everyone for a prolonged period. That's what Karel Vuursteen did when he took over as chief executive of the Heineken breweries in the early 1990s.

Heineken was then the world's biggest international beer company, after Anheuser-Busch. But its performance had been slipping, and Vuursteen was not alone in thinking the company's sociable, paternalistic culture had bred a degree of complacency. We were working with Heineken at the time, on a project to introduce "the new Heineken spirit." It was intended to make the company more market focused, aggressive, entrepreneurial, and growth oriented.

It was a hard sell in the easygoing Heineken culture. But when Vuursteen started making his presentation at our workshops, he got attention. He is a big figure, larger than life, an extrovert with a wonderful sense of humor. However, in his first months at Heineken, he was all distant formality, and his talks were aimed to scare the pants off his executives. He would speak with a background picture of fish swimming in the sea. The fish were labeled as beer companies, one of them Heineken. There was a big pair of jaws, unlabeled, at the edge of the picture. Vuursteen would discuss the fish and describe their market shares, and inevitably, someone in the group would ask what the jaws on the edge represented. He would slowly walk over to the overhead and say, quietly and dramatically, "Anheuser-Busch." (Dropping the tone of your voice, as Karel Vuursteen did, is an effective social technique used by many leaders. People are highly tuned to tonal variation.)

Given Heineken's family-based ownership, it's safe to say no one in the company had been worried about any takeover. But after that moment, which Vuursteen reproduced in ten separate workshops, we often said you could feel the assembled hearts start to flutter. From then on, they were running scared. This was precisely his intention.

Vuursteen maintained his social distance until his people all recognized that their world was more threatening than they had thought. As the next ten years brought consistent growth in revenues, profitability, margins, and share price for Heineken, Vuursteen gradually shifted his balance toward his natural métier, closeness. He would eat his lunch in the cafeteria, socialize with employees, and be the life of the party. Any Heineken executive, manager, or worker would tell you what a great guy he is. And he is, but you might not have guessed it at the beginning.

Adding Objectivity

Distance is also required when a leader wants to step back for a better perspective on a complex, multifaceted issue. The leader's job is to look out for all the stakeholders in an organization, and that can't be done if the leader is too close to any one group of them. Mired in a complex situation, the leader must rise above it to understand it. Preserving distance may be the only way to see the full picture.

This was a lesson learned by Niall FitzGerald in his early days as chief executive of Unilever. At the time, the company was working on a new detergent, Persil Power, to compete with Procter & Gamble's hugely successful Tide. There was just one problem: Persil Power ate holes in the clothes it was washing. It kept doing it, even in Unilever's own tests, but the company's development team somehow ignored this fact. The team was committed to the project, and FitzGerald was determined to stand by his troops.

Just before the launch, P&G's people actually warned Unilever not to go ahead. They had tested Persil Power themselves and had seen how it destroyed clothing, and they were worried about the potential impact its spectacular failure might have on P&G's own laundry detergent business. Unilever's team responded by arguing that P&G was just trying to sabotage their launch, and went ahead. Sure enough, the new detergent ate holes in customers' clothes. It was a complete disaster.

Looking back, FitzGerald knows he was guilty of getting too close to his development team at a huge cost to his marketers, his investors, and his company's reputation. "That was the popular place to be, but I should not have been there," he says now. Leadership, he believes, isn't necessarily about standing with the troops in the trenches. Sometimes you have to be up on a hill, surveying the whole field. "I should have stood back, cool and detached," he told us, "and watched out for the customer."

Too Close, Too Soon

We have all been irritated by the gushing salesperson who uses first names with customers from the start, the overfriendly wait-ress who gives unwanted advice, or the gung-ho corporate recruit who boasts about great teamwork he has not yet experienced. When closeness is premature or inauthentic, distance is required.

We know a young MBA graduate, from a top U.S. business school. He is thirty-five years old and very bright. He dived into his first position convinced that sociability was the key to success. To demonstrate that he was one of the boys, he took his people out drinking and got drunk with them. He took them to a strip club downtown. He got very chummy with everyone. Then he discov-ered that the sales director, an older man, had been taking kick-backs from customers. The managing director needed to assert dis-tance to handle this situation, but it was by now all but impossible.

When leaders are establishing goals, objectives, and the rules of the game, distance is essential. Norms, values, and standards need to be communicated as nonnegotiable. These are the bedrock on which operations are built. This can only be done effectively early in a leadership relationship, with as much distance and for-mality as possible.

When Pete Goss was training raw crews for the BT Challenge round-the-world race, he established his rules from the start. The coming weeks would be stressful and sometimes dangerous; there could be no debate about who was to do what, or how. Everyone would do any assigned job, without shirking, or the toilets would not get cleaned and the bilge would not be pumped. No discussion or debate was allowed. Closeness would come later.

We've seen this work in corporate situations, where the leader says up front, "Let me make things clear. You will deliver on your numbers." That's said from full distance, with no debate or discussion. This is the way it's going to be, period. Then the leader gets into a discussion of how people are going to do it, with considerable back and forth, suggestions from the group, and a growing sense of warmth and collegiality: we're all in this together; the team will make the goal. For the leader, the pattern is often this: be distant when you tell them what to do; be close when you talk about how.

Getting Closer

While we have so far highlighted leaders with a predisposition to distance, others have a default mode of closeness. Bill Burns, for example, is better at closeness than distance, and he recognizes that. "I tell people the way I see it," he told us. "There's a consistency—they know where they stand with me, good or bad." Burns acknowledges that "there's a soft side to it. I am interested in people. I have a very good memory. If people tap me on the shoulder, and I haven't seen them for years, I can often remember something to do with them or their family or whatever. And I can help people get through a complex situation and reach a conclusion." Small wonder that his colleagues recognize Bill as someone they can easily and confidently confide in.

Of course, Burns's memory is not restricted to the names of the spouses of employees: "I also remember products and markets—people may feel 'Oh no, he's remembered we were off the boil last year. Are we back on track now?' So there's an edge to it. There's an understanding of the business."

Whatever the mix, Burns's strategy works. He drove through a program to focus activities and reduce costs within the pharma division, making sweeping changes along the way. In sharp contrast to many of Birt's initiatives at the BBC, the move was managed with remarkably little rancor and few disputes.

As with distance, there are many occasions when leaders find it appropriate to use closeness to strengthen bonds with their followers.

One of the most obvious occasions is when trying to build a team. Team building depends on knowing the abilities and person-alities of the individual members. This can't be done without get-ting close enough to know what motivates them. The leader also has to figure out how to differentiate their approach. Motivating Joe to perform well may involve a different set of signals and incentives than is necessary for Susan. And since the members must bond with each other to identify as a team, team building often involves getting out of the workplace to more social settings where work barriers are effectively removed and closeness comes naturally.

David Gardner, while head of Electronic Arts' European opera-tions, may hold a record of sorts in team building away from the office. Gardner took his entire European workforce—almost one thousand people—to Club Med for a four-day stay. Gardner is an American, and at first his people were skeptical, bordering on cyn-ical, about the whole idea. We just don't do things like that, they sniffed. But the trip was such a roaring success that the next year the staff clamored to know where they were going now. Gardner's answer: "Nowhere." Such jaunts were to celebrate success, he told them, and the numbers this year weren't up to expectations. His answer illustrates a more general point about team building. While we have stressed the significance of closeness, it is not enough on its own. Closeness may be a necessary condition, but it is not a sufficient one. Effective teams also need clarity about tasks and purpose, and this comes from the leader too.

Closeness is also essential when coaching or giving intensive help. Good coaching begins with understanding the goals, motives, ambitions, and emotions of others, to help them to take more responsibility for their development.

When Rick Dobbis landed in Europe to run what was already a successful business for PolyGram, some of his friends were worried about how he would react to the culture shock. They were concerned that his Brooklyn background would come through too much—that he would feel he needed to stamp his authority on the organization. Instead, he chose the wiser strategy of listening to his new colleagues and then demonstrating that he could help them. He used the closeness established by listening to coach them in the techniques he had learned in the United States—things like establishing a separate budget price label and moving repertoire around Europe.

To understand what really makes their people tick, leaders must find out personal information about individuals. They must learn their histories, goals, and dreams, even delve into their regrets and disappointments. They must learn peoples' names and the names of their spouses and children. They must find out their causes and pastimes while also sharing their own values and passions. If the leader isn't genuinely close, they may well only hear what people think they want to hear.

When Gareth left PolyGram, Rick Dobbis bought him a book, a history of Brooklyn, very much the place of his origins. He had inscribed it: "Many great things come out of Brooklyn. Funny, you could have come from there yourself." It was a great compliment to receive, a truly personalized gift.

One of the best settings for developing such closeness is while traveling together, sharing food and drink. Some leaders even invite people to their homes. Early in his tenure at the BBC, Greg Dyke took the entire top executive team on a trip from London to Leeds. They were going to visit the offices of BBC North, where the people felt beleaguered. The BBC gets progressively less popular as you travel north in England, and the Leeds office seldom saw any visitors from headquarters. Dyke wanted not only to strengthen his executive team but to establish some closeness between the two offices.

He told the group to travel in twos and threes, and each duo or trio was assigned to visit another BBC local radio station along the way. The members naturally got closer to each other, learned things they hadn't known about the organization, and formed bonds with people in unexpected places. When they got to Leeds, staffers who had seen hardly any top executives were treated to the whole top team, walking around the building almost like a conga line. Dyke presided affably over a joint staff meeting, successfully hiding the fact that he was on the point of fainting from a toothache.

The Genuine Article

Authenticity is especially sensitive when a leader is expressing closeness. If it isn't genuinely felt, followers will sooner or later sense that fact and feel that they have been tricked.

We once consulted to a leading hospital administrator in Boston who was superb at collecting soft data. He got to know everyone in the hospital. He knew the kitchen staff, porters, security men, even the parking attendants—as well as the surgeons, nurses, and doctors—and he was very good at putting in the time and effort to walk the corridors and wards. He was clearly doing his homework, because he knew people's names before he met them. It was flattering, and people would tell him whatever he wanted to know. However, he made a big mistake. He did all that as part of his situation sensing in his first six months on the job, and then he stopped.

For his people, it was as if he weren't interested anymore. His authenticity was diminished, and a lot of his credibility, too. The critical point here is that situation sensing is not a one-off episode—leaders need to review their knowledge base about people and the organization. Leadership may ultimately be about overarching purpose, but it's constantly about people and relationships.

And it is a two-way thing. To become authentically close to people, you can't merely probe into their sensitive places. In exchange, you must also show them quite a lot of yourself. At a leadership event for senior partners in a global professional services firm, we invited the partners to tell their colleagues something about themselves that other people in the room did not know. The range of behavior was amazing; some ducked the task by trotting out banalities: "My favorite color is orange;" others made real disclosures: "My wife and I are having marital therapy," "I failed my professional exams—twice." If you don't disclose, it is very hard to express closeness. But you must be honest about it. If your people start comparing notes and find discrepancies, your credibility is shot—and they will stop being honest with you, too.

Closeness is about showing positive emotions. This may involve rewarding success and consoling people who stumble. Optimism is contagious; pessimism inspires fear and doubt, and tends to be a self-fulfilling prophecy. Those who take risks should be encouraged, even if the risk doesn't pay off every time. Few people hit a home run the first time at bat.

Opening the Door to Closeness

Closeness can be staged. But this cannot be achieved mechanically. The opportunities for closeness must fit the style and personality of the leader and the situation they face. The techniques used must match the people the leader is working with.

This was brought home to us when we worked on team building with the researchers at a pharmaceutical company. We went through a standard routine, trying to get them to share soft data about each other and so forth, but none of it worked. We finally set up a series of seminars where they could talk about their research. That was what really fascinated them—that was what they wanted to know about each other. After all, they were scientists.

Leaders often stage occasions for closeness, creating a kind of cocoon in which they and their people can let down their hair.

Before he went to the BBC, for instance, Greg Dyke ran a commercial television station, London Weekend. As he would do again at the BBC, he created a "leadership group" for the company and worked hard to make the members feel like a team. Among his techniques was a series of breakfast meetings for the group, with invited speakers—including, on separate occasions, both of us. The game was that after the twenty-minute presentation, Dyke would lead the team in demolishing the speaker and the speech. It was a tough, funny ritual, a form of intellectual bearbaiting, often brilliantly done. Egged on by Dyke, the team members tried to outdo each other in outrageous wit, and bonded tightly in the laughter. Even for the victim, it was fun—after the first shock.

While grand gestures, like David Gardner's Club Med excursion, are effective and memorable, it is even more important to do small things more often. Leaving all the bonding to an annual occasion is like trying to repair a marriage on summer vacation. Small social rituals, such as coffee and cookies on Monday morning, can become useful habits—so long as they don't become routine.

Even in organizations that rely on hierarchy as a controlling mechanism, establishing closeness is a highly effective leadership device. Great military leaders succeed by winning not just respect from their troops, but devotion. They win it by talking to them in their own language and showing that they care. General George Patton talked his men across Europe, basically telling them, "The only thing that matters to me is the American soldier." And when Lord Nelson was hit by shrapnel in battle, he thought he was dying. One of the ship's surgeons left the wounded man he was working on and rushed to help the admiral, but Nelson said, "I'll take my turn alongside my brave men." That was unfakable, authenticity under fire—and the sailors loved him for it.[13]

Consider another classic hierarchical context—a steelworks—where safety, even life itself, rests on the power of hierarchical relations. We observed a first-time supervisor who during work insisted on respect for his role, but during coffee and meal breaks established closeness through gentle, and not so gentle, humor about which baseball and football teams his subordinates supported.

How to Use Bandwidth

The hard part for leaders is when and how to shift the balance from distance toward closeness, or vice versa. The balance is always shifting—often gradually, sometimes abruptly.

Some manage the movement between closeness and distance very effectively. David Prosser, for example, is no smooth, City of London business type. He's a big man from industrial South Wales, with an accent to match. Prosser does closeness well. He is chief executive of Legal & General, one of Europe's most successful insurance companies, an organization whose culture is warm and intimate, focusing on after-work drinks and friendly parties for departing executives. Prosser radiates warmth at such events and is invariably courteous, polite, and pleasant in one-on-one meetings with his people. But he can switch to distance with devastating effect, politely and firmly pointing out any shortfalls.

His use of distance is all the more effective because of the warmth he generates. At a cocktail party, for instance, a rather excitable sales manager was boasting how good the company is at cross-selling products. In his low voice, Prosser intervened: "We may be good, but we're not good enough." The ice refroze in the glasses. Everyone took the point: they can do better and are expected to do better.

In general, it is fairly easy to signal the shift from distance to closeness. A smile, an easier manner, a pleasant social remark give people permission to relax and a sign that, for now at least, authority is resting and closeness is appropriate. However, many people find it more difficult to make the switch to distance. The very personable research leader, for instance, turned abruptly into a savage critic and left her followers shaken and betrayed.

Among the leaders we studied, there were a number of ways in which they shifted the balance.

The first commonly used technique we have observed is to manage the transition to distance by telling people what's going to happen to them. Nigel Morris, cofounder and former COO of Capital One, acknowledges that he feels "a little like a chameleon, one minute pally and chummy, the next driven and hard edged." As he told us, "If you are too enigmatic, it's scary for people.

Predictability is important even if it is harsh. I tend to give people warning by saying, 'Look, Rob, the other Nigel is coming out'—to signal that I am going to change."

Of course, such emotional displays aren't simply a case of on or off, black or white, open or closed. Some sophisticated leaders keep people on their toes by using conflicting signals. This technique is best used when the basic strategy is to impose distance.

We saw this for ourselves in our first meeting with the chief executive of a large investment bank. We were to see him over lunch with two of his senior executives, who went to brief him on the meeting just before it was to happen. He clearly gave them an uncomfortable half hour, and they retreated from his office to where we were waiting with their tails between their legs. We went with them to the private dining room for lunch. When the CEO didn't turn up, we began eating. Two courses went by, and we were all increasingly nervous, thinking that if he did come, we'd work hard to try and make it work. When he finally showed up, he was pleasant and cordial; we had a great conversation. But the chief executive had gained an edge by his display of authority, and we may well have conceded more points than we intended. All told, it was a classic example of a leader using distance to keep people on their toes.

The Risks of Getting It Wrong

When a leader fails to make the right moves between distance and closeness, to keep adjusting when conditions change, he or she becomes less effective. The organization doesn't necessarily fall apart. We have all seen companies with leaders ranging from mediocre to inept that somehow manage to fumble along for years.

And one way or another, the leader who gets the balance wrong always fails to achieve authenticity. Consider these cases:

When too much closeness gets in the way of addressing performance issues. Remember the young manager who went drinking with his people and later found that one of them was taking kickbacks? The problem is rarely so extreme; in fact, most leaders can handle such severe lapses even if they have overdone closeness. But being too close almost always impedes addressing problems of mediocrity. In such cases, when a manager tries to assume distance with his or her buddy, he can slip the whole issue with a joke, as fat Jack Falstaff did with Prince Hal. By getting too close, the manager has forfeited his authenticity.

When closeness is premature. We have all met people who come on too strong when joining a team and try to assume a closeness they have not yet earned. It's far better to overdo distance first, like a teacher with a new class.

When leaders fail to recognize their accountability. If a manager focuses too much on closeness as the team leader and moving spirit of the operation, he may lose the authenticity of his mandate to generate performance and be accountable for the outcome. Leadership is not about being nice. Even while being close, the leader must reserve a degree of himself; both he and his followers must feel the edgy potential of distance. In the end, authority derives from the overriding cause or goal of the organization; it is as the steward of that cause that the leader can impose distance even on people he is close to.

When leaders are distant even though closeness is appropriate. By the nature of their role, leaders are often required to focus on factors outside the organization. They spend a lot of time talking with investors, analysts, the press, customers, and government, rather than facing inward to the organization. As a result, they are often perceived to be literally distant as well as socially distant, and then lose touch with what is going on. They are cut off from just the sources of soft data that would make them effective leaders.

We once saw graffiti in an executive lavatory that told us all we needed to know about that particular CEO: "What is the difference between God and the chief executive? God is everywhere. The chief is everywhere but here." Such senior executives are constantly surprised when key employees leave, or when the sales force falls "suddenly" short of its target.

That kind of remoteness can be seductive. It permits a chief executive to argue—witness the Enron, Tyco, and WorldCom fiascos—that since he didn't know what was going on, he is not responsible. As the leader, of course you are responsible. It is the final outcome, the overriding cause of the enterprise that gives you your authenticity.

When a leader finds a good technique but pushes it too far. We have all known managers who came into an organization, established admirable distance and authority, and then went too far with decisions that were perceived as brutal or damaging to the organization's long-term good. However, it is just as easy to lose authenticity with ill-judged closeness.

It should never be forgotten that like some other aspects of management, leadership is a skill. Those who aspire to be very effective leaders constantly practice and hone their skills. Using social distance, as we have shown, is a critical leadership skill. But like every skill, it can also be overplayed.

Once, at a well-known ad agency, we witnessed a case study in how easy it is to push too far and so lose impact. Before the annual departmental Christmas party, the manager told us he planned to single out five outstanding performers, tell what they had done, and give each of them a prize. This all sounded fine. But when he did it, he didn't stop at five. He kept going, praising more and more people and passing out the prizes.

At first, excitement built in the room. But as it became plain that everyone in the department, some fifty people, were all going to get a prize, the ceremony began to degenerate. As he ran out of real heroes, the manager was reading from notes, and the notes were increasingly thin. The people being praised weren't feeling good about it, and the real heroes felt their prizes were cheapened. The event had felt genuine through the first five or six names, and then less and less authentic until it became a sham, a trick that backfired.

We can see that using social distance skillfully is a special type of situation sensing, reading when to get close, when to be more distant, and then knowing which behaviors are most appropriate. This is a critical leadership skill.

There is one more critical competence to explore. In the next chapter, we examine why communicating with care is so important in the leadership relationship.

SEVEN

Communicate—with Care

I T HAS BECOME COMMONPLACE to read in the leadership literature that effective leaders are good communicators. They are, but there is more to it. Skillful leaders ensure that they use the right *mode* of communication. This requires a fine appreciation of the message, the context, the people you wish to communicate with, as well as your own personal strengths and weaknesses. In effect, thinking carefully about your mode of communication is a miniature case study in how you can effectively *be yourself, in context, with skill.*[1]

Leaders need to consider, for example, whether their strength lies in one-to-one meetings, a small group, or a large-scale speech. Each context requires quite distinctive presentational skills. And clearly, each encounter may be different according to context.

A famous Harvard Business School case documents the meticulous care and preparation that Orit Gadiesh, vice-chairman of the consulting firm Bain and Company, invested in an important speech to her colleagues at the company in the early 1990s.[2] At the time, the firm was suffering from low morale, an issue that Gadiesh sought to address. Among the factors she considered were the appropriate balance of fact and emotion, recent accomplishments and future challenges, personal anecdotes, and shared experiences. She knew that how she communicated as their leader would have an important effect on how the message was received. Above all, Gadiesh considered how to build a sense of collective pride without having a large group of independent-minded personalities feel they had been inappropriately commanded.

Choosing the Channel

Think again about Greg Dyke's careful staging of his magic act, Thomas Sattelberger's use of his eyes in small meetings, or Simon Gulliford's road shows. Leaders must consider whether they invest the same attention to this key task. Do they communicate with care?

Communication is personal. While face-to-face communication will always be important for leaders, it is also necessary for them to consider how to connect directly and effectively with larger audiences. When John Major succeeded Margaret Thatcher as prime minister in the United Kingdom, he was widely expected to lose the first election that he fought. At the beginning of the campaign, he delivered a series of set-piece speeches from big platforms complete with glass autocue. The reception was underwhelming. The setting did not complement his understated, modest style. Halfway through the campaign, he changed tack. He began a series of street corner speeches delivered impromptu from a makeshift stand—his soapbox—with a handheld microphone. The setting captured his "ordinary man in the street" style far more effectively. The speeches were captured on all the major TV channels and duly broadcast to 30 million voters. He won the election. Many commentators saw this presentational shift as the key turning point in the campaign. Suddenly, Major began to connect with people.

The analogies with the 2004 Bush-Kerry presidential contest are tantalizing. Bush loved being out on the stump. It was his preferred milieu. Kerry, by general consent, did well in the more staged atmosphere of the TV debates. Only very late on in the campaign, too late for him, did he seem to connect with the electorate in more informal settings.

Organizations that we work with recognize the increasing significance of the internal and external communication agenda. Indeed, the communication function has risen in importance over recent years. At their best, communications professionals are able to complement the interpersonal interactions of leaders with sophisticated use of new and old channels: videoconferencing, the Internet, printed publications, advertising, and so on. All of these can be extremely effective so long as the machine does not take over. But leaders must retain their authenticity. Remember, for example, the care taken by Peter Brabeck in considering the appropriateness of his photograph in a mountaineering outfit for the Nestlé water publication.

Lower down the organization, channel selection is just as important. We have observed and interviewed on many occasions a senior social worker in a tough inner-city borough. Dave's team is hard to run: it contains political radicals, several varieties of feminists, ruthless careerists, and self-styled anarchists. Formal meetings are a nightmare—they can rapidly deteriorate into an unproductive exchange between entrenched positions. Dave understands this completely and elects instead to take small groups of staff to a friendly local bar where with humor, intellect, and informality, he communicates the high standards of professional practice he requires.

Leadership Narrative

Clearly, communication is also a matter of content. The mistake many leaders make is to assume that followers can be engaged primarily through rational analysis and straightforward assertion of the facts.[3] From school through college and into work, this is the way we are encouraged to convince others of the merits of our case. But this approach—on its own—is rarely successful in *energizing* others.

When, for example, were you last excited by a lengthy, data-packed PowerPoint presentation? Or a detailed set of fact-laden briefing papers? Besides the predictable disinterest that these approaches evoke, the problem is often further compounded by individuals using their hierarchical authority to ensure that others are sufficiently "convinced" by the merits of their case. This may pass for management in some organizations, but it is certainly not leadership.

In order to properly engage others, leaders need to construct a compelling narrative. They must find a way of looking at the world that allows others not only to understand their role in it but also to be excited by it. This does not mean rejecting reasonable analysis. Rather, effective leaders bring their case alive through rich examples, personal experiences, analogies, and stories.[4]

Why are these devices so powerful as a means for leadership communication? There are several reasons. First, a convincing story is a means of engaging others, and, as we have stressed, leadership is a relationship. Good stories draw people in. They present a puzzle that must be solved, a challenge that must be overcome, a quest, if you will. And they are effective because ultimately they allow others to draw their own conclusions.

Second, well-chosen use of personal experiences can help followers to identify with leaders. Personal anecdote and experience are an important means of reducing social distance—and revealing authentic biography. By using familiar episodes or contexts from daily life, leaders are often able to better connect with others on the basis of shared experience.

Third, by personalizing their communications—through anecdotes, analogies, and humor, for example—leaders are able to reveal more of who they are. And the more leaders reveal their own emotions (skillfully), the more they evoke an emotional reaction in others. Jack Welch, the celebrated former CEO of General Electric, used this technique to connect with people, frequently recalling stories from his childhood and early adult life to illustrate key messages. But we prefer another example.

We have watched yachtsman Pete Goss give presentations to rooms full of hardened executives over recent years. He is a masterly storyteller. One story he tells is of his remarkable rescue of fellow competitor Raphael Dinelli—who was near death in a round-the-world yacht race in the eye of a fierce storm. Another tale recounts his development of a revolutionary giant catamaran, Team Philips. They each exemplify the power of a good story.

Both stories present a challenge that effectively draws the audience in. How can he possibly succeed in the rescue in such fierce conditions? Will Raphael still be alive by the time Pete reaches him? Is it really possible to develop a catamaran that is effectively the size of a small marina rather than another boat? Will it survive in a "perfect storm"? Will Pete raise enough funds to keep the project going?

As each dramatic story unfolds, Pete weaves in and out personal anecdotes of familiar, mundane daily routines with which others can easily connect—the routines of eating, sleeping, and, yes, even using the toilet when the boat is awash with water. He talks of the vital support of his wife, the daily camaraderie of his friends.

Finally, the stories enable Pete to reveal his emotions. On first rescuing Raphael, he talks movingly of their embrace—and of his eyes: "I shall never forget them . . . I had no idea what depth of emotion and gratitude they can convey." On abandoning the giant catamaran—fatally damaged at sea—he confides that he and all his crew members wept openly as the boat slid silently into the night.

By the close, Pete has connected powerfully with his audience—enabling them to share some of his experiences and draw their own conclusions about the personal challenges of leadership.

Authentic Storytelling

Are there recipes for this kind of communication? There are certainly some basic guidelines for an effective story—in terms of structure, pace, and style, for example. We also know that impactful narratives often draw upon ancient stories in their imagery and tone. Think, for instance, of the way in which Steve Jobs deployed the David and Goliath imagery in his depiction of the battle between Apple and IBM. Exactly the same analogy was used by Richard Branson as he established Virgin in competition with British Airways; and, indeed, by the new generation of low-cost carriers as they fought the established airlines.

Effective communication must be authentic. The use of example, anecdote, or story must fit the context and the moment; and it must feel real—not borrowed from a recipe. Used most effectively, these devices are woven into the fabric of day-to-day interaction rather than added on as an afterthought.

Skillful communication is also a matter of pace and timing. Pace, tempo, and orchestration are at the heart of successful leadership communication. Too fast, and the messages become scrambled, or they may not fit the context. Too slow, and there is a danger of frustration and disengagement. The leader's task is to read and understand the rhythm of the organization and then work out what must change and at what speed—and what, at all costs, must stay the same.

Of Tortoises and Hares

Communicating with care is about more than content, style, and storytelling. It's also about timing and pace. Music isn't just about notes—as one jazz musician put it, "Just listen to the notes I don't play." Indeed, executives in the Wharton Business School International Forum Music and Leadership Program who are asked to learn how to conduct a quartet say that this is what most resembles their challenges at work.

Consider the following two cases. We've made them anonymous to make it more interesting for you because we want you to guess what happened next. The first story is about a company founded in the early years of the twentieth century, building on the new technologies that had emerged, combining knowledge of electricity and communications. By the early 1960s, the company had become a large conglomerate with businesses in heavy and light engineering: power generation, defense, medical electronics, and consumer durables.

It pursued a conservative strategy—never putting all its eggs in one basket, combined with tight (some thought stifling), centralized financial controls. Many managers felt this produced a bureaucratic and risk-averse organization, ill equipped to respond quickly to new opportunities. Nevertheless, the company grew. By the 1960s, revenues were around £10 billion, and it had £1 billion in cash. Its risk aversion, however, made it unpopular with the capital market. It underperformed the FTSE share index in all but four years between 1987 and 1996.

But by the late 1990s, the company was ripe for change and new leadership. A new chief executive was appointed. He already had a considerable reputation as a business leader who was not afraid of radically changing organizations. The new leader speedily set about changing things. He strengthened the board with a former investment banker and embarked on root-and-branch strategic change. He left behind the risk-averse strategies of the past and sought to reposition the company in the rapidly growing market for telecommunications equipment. An accelerated disposals program culminated in the sale of the corporation's defense business.

Together with these bold moves, the organization embarked on a major culture change effort. The aim was to communicate the new strategic imperatives to the workforce. Working with the HR director, the new CEO identified core values—such as passion and pride, high velocity, and a radical outlook—around which to build a new organization. The formula was classic change management, driven by inspiring leadership. The markets looked favorably on the company, and it became a hot stock. Employees came to believe that the share price could double—a level at which their options would vest. People were truly focused on the share price and motivated to achieve the target. With a strong tailwind of enthusiasm, the CEO embarked on an acquisition strategy to develop global capability. There followed two major purchases in the United States: one for just over $2 billion and another for $4.2 billion.

"Our mission is to make this organization one of the world's leading telecommunication and information management companies in the most dynamic and exciting market sections of the twenty-first century. We will achieve this by building a culture in which we will all share in the success of the new organization," proclaimed the bullish CEO in 2000.

Let's leave the story there—and you can think what happened next—while we consider another rather different case.

This is a professional services partnership operating in a specialized quasi-legal financial restructuring business. It is blue chip, with an impressive top-of-the-range brand image. At the time we ran across the organization, its revenues were around $750 million and came from a variety of activities. These included big financial restructuring work, acting either for banks, bondholders, or, occasionally, management; highly specialized corporate turnaround activities requiring detailed sector knowledge; and restructuring or liquidating small and medium-sized enterprises. The general picture looks very rosy. Revenues are growing—the business is on target to double in size within five years. Profitability is good—with profits per partner very high when benchmarked against others. In the big-ticket work, growth is still strong and highly profitable. Talent within the company follows the money, and the company's best brains gravitate toward the big-name, high-profile work.

Meanwhile, beneath the surface, problems lurk. Smaller, nimble boutique players are entering the corporate market. They see the blue-chip market leader as slow moving and perhaps a little complacent. The harsh truth is that in the small and medium-sized enterprise market, which remains about 40 percent of revenues, the partnership has been losing market share consistently for several years. Lower-cost regional players or big players committed to relationship marketing have been gaining market share.

Something needs to be done. So the partnership leader sponsors an internal study to be carried out by a wise owl of the business. After conducting eighty internal interviews and many more with customers, he recommends a radical change. The small and medium-sized sector business needs new leadership—someone who will pull together a somewhat demoralized group, give it clear direction, and begin to regain market share.

The leader ponders options. There seem to be no obvious candidates for this dramatic turnaround work. Eventually, after much discussion with his senior colleagues, he turns to an experienced but younger partner. The young partner has a record of introducing innovative people processes into the partnership, especially focused on learning and development for younger talent. But he does not have a reputation as a dedicated hitter.

The young partner begins well. There are lots of meetings to consult the older partners who have had some success in local markets, and, gradually, he engages the directors and managers beneath partner level. There are subcommittees and task forces to examine structural options, channel management, new-talent development, and brand issues. This generates much lively talk and some cynicism—"We've tried this before and it didn't work." The new leader does his best to bring this to the surface before moving on with the necessary changes, but there is a growing sense that there is too much talk, consultation, and consensus building.

In partner workshops, there is a rumble of disquiet, demanding decisive action.

Let's leave that story and return to our dynamic telecommunication business.

Hare Today . . .

The first half of 2000 saw rapid growth and strong earnings. The share price reached an all-time high. It had worked. But then, in 2001 the U.S. market for telecommunications fell away as entrants into the newly deregulated markets began to fail. The European market was stronger, but even here many of the large players were hampered by the effects of paying large fees for third-generation cell-phone licenses. As a consequence, they delayed investment in network infrastructure. Another blow for the organization.

In the second quarter of 2001, the company announced a poor sales outlook and a disastrous 50 percent fall in expected operating profit. The share price went into free fall. By the third quarter, the shares were relegated from the FTSE 100 index, and the CEO and chairman (a former Executive of the Year) resigned. Quite soon the share became virtually valueless as the company's enormous debts were restructured. A blue chip with large cash reserves had been destroyed. The organization was Marconi Corporation.

Let's return to our professional services firm. The calls to action were heard. A new management team of young talent was put together. They are working now on renewing the talent base, rebuilding relationships with regional bankers. The problems aren't all resolved, but there is an increasing feeling that the business is moving in the right direction. One or two senior people have joined from the competition. They saw where the action was and wanted to be a part of it. Some of the cynics have left, more may follow.

Communication of the vision remains vital to long term success, but the careful hard work has begun. The organization is Pricewater-houseCoopers Business Recovery Services regional practice. As we write, it is regaining market share, spirits are high, and people are engaged.

As with the tortoise and the hare, our two cases illustrate that a more gradual and carefully crafted change process can prove ulti-mately far more successful. In the first case, new leaders arrived with impressive track records. Energy was initially created around a dramatic new vision in which all were to share in future success. Aggressive acquisition-based expansion was rapidly pursued. In the process, the traditional base of the business was lost, and care-fully developed disciplines were blown away. When the market shifted, a great company was undermined. In the second case, a quieter, less-striking figure took the reins of leadership, carefully consulted with colleagues, adjusted the business, rebuilt customer relationships, and began to build a team dedicated to the newly emerging vision. The hare is badly wounded; the tortoise is alive and well and making steady progress.

Perhaps inevitably, the hares will always draw more of our attention. They did so spectacularly in the 1990s—and we are still recovering from the corporate collapses that often followed in their wake. It is not surprising, perhaps, that quiet, moderately paced leaders have become more popular.

The Myth of Fast Executive Reflexes

Time and again, leaders face the difficult question of pace and timing. And with performance pressures increasing, many business leaders, in particular, feel driven to show their impact faster and faster. They feel the need to communicate, in effect, that they have all the answers. Yet recent research suggests that this represents one of the defining characteristics of high-profile failures.

Professor Sydney Finkelstein from the Tuck School of Business at Dartmouth College has made a study of "spectacularly unsuccessful" people.[5] He defines these as individuals able to take world-renowned businesses and make them almost worthless—destroying jobs and shareholder value on a vast scale. This describes Marconi perfectly—but there are parallels, as Finkelstein points out, with Wolfgang Schmitt, chairman and CEO of Rubbermaid, Roger Smith at GM (EDS), and Dennis Kozlowski of Tyco, to name just three. All took strongly performing companies and propelled them down dead ends of various sorts.

It is hard, of course, not to be impressed by individuals who seem able to focus swiftly on what's important, make sense out of complexity, demonstrate deep familiarity with the relevant facts, and act decisively. In fact, this stereotypical portrait of executive behavior remains an aspiration for many at work. Leaders who take on this ideal relish the opportunity to make snap decisions and issue orders at high speed. What's more, their colleagues often feel reassured by their decisiveness—despite the fact that they *know* they can't have all the answers.

But as Syd Finkelstein cautions,

The problem with this picture of executive competence is that it is really a fraud. In a world where business conditions are constantly changing and innovations often seem to be the only constant, no one can "have all the answers" for long. Leaders who are invariably crisp and decisive tend to settle issues so quickly that they have no opportunity to grasp the ramifications. Worse, because these leaders need to feel they already have all the answers, they have no way to learn *new* answers. Their instinct, whenever something truly important is at stake, is to push for rapid closure, allowing no periods of uncertainty, even when uncertainty is appropriate.[6]

Those who act too quickly and with unrealistic certainty suffer from another problem. They cease to receive useful feedback or input from others. Colleagues of Wolfgang Schmitt at Rubbermaid claimed that he didn't listen or accept advice and suggestions. In the end, there were "few left who will dare to disagree with him anyway."[7] Ultimately, then, another speed trap is silence. With pressure to achieve things fast, individuals often feel the need to "just do it," to get on with the task and talk about the problems later. But as two Harvard academics, Leslie Perlow and Stephanie Williams, have recently shown, the conspiracy of silence that this creates can demotivate, create anger and resentment between colleagues, undermine creativity, and reduce productivity.[8]

An exemplar of the tortoise approach is Franz Humer. During his eight years at Roche, he led a dramatic reshaping to focus around the core businesses of pharmaceuticals and diagnostics. But he was initially mindful of the dangers of trying to accomplish too much too soon. Many wanted Humer to dispose of the troubled vitamins business as soon as he arrived. But he was aware of the early resistance that this might have created inside the company—and the problems it might cause in his ambition for change elsewhere in the business.

Not long after he arrived at Roche, the company was hitting the headlines—but for all the wrong reasons. Reports focused on falling market share, a poor product pipeline, a price-fixing scandal with massive penalties in both the United States and Europe, and the threat of a takeover by Novartis. Looking back, Humer reflects that his communication task at the time was to convince people that things were not as bad as they appeared. He had to remind people— in the face of negative change—of the fundamental continuities that were the strengths of the business, to communicate what he now describes as an almost unrealistic optimism.

More recently, the company has been reporting healthy profits, and growth rates ahead of the market. Bad news, says Humer. "Now I must remind my colleagues that we are not as good as we think we are!" This story illustrates the fine line that all leaders must tread as they communicate to their followers and, in effect, answer the question "How are we doing?" For those sitting on top of complex organizations facing fast change, the answer to this question is rarely simple. Getting it right requires situation sensing and communication of the highest order.

Evolution Versus Revolution

Perhaps no company better illustrates the trade-offs between more evenly paced evolution and fast-paced revolution than the food giant Nestlé (voted by one magazine as the best organization for leaders worldwide). Indeed, CEO Peter Brabeck has made a very public point of addressing this tension as a central part of his personal leadership challenge.[9]

Nestlé is the world's biggest food company. Nearly 150-years old, it operates in every country on earth, selling thousands of products. It has 260,000 employees, and with brands such as Nestlé, Perrier, Friskies, and Kit-Kat, holds a dominant position in many fast-moving consumer goods markets.

During the technology-fueled growth of the 1990s, Nestlé was often described as "dull," "boring," "a lame duck," and "a dinosaur." But when the dot-com bubble burst, the virtues of Nestlé's long-term commitment to sustainable, evolutionary growth became more evident.

Indeed, Brabeck, like his predecessors, has continued to emphasize the firm's "untouchables"—those aspects of the business that should never change. The *Economist* labeled Brabeck "a dedicated enemy of fashion."[10] As he explained, "One of the main jobs of the leader is to determine what aspects of the company you want to keep. You have to be clear about why the company has been successful in the past, and how you are going to keep those fundamentals from breaking down or disappearing."

These persisting values are captured in the Nestlé *Leadership and Management Principles,* which Brabeck produced upon becoming CEO in 1997, after thirty years with the company. Among these principles are the importance of people, products, and brands (rather than technology); a long-term view of business development; and a decentralized philosophy that pushes decision making out in the organization and as close to local markets as possible.

Clearly, this does not mean that Nestlé is not changing. Rather, there is an institutional preference for gradual but continuous evolutionary change. Again, as Brabeck has publicly remarked, one-off dramatic change is traumatic, disruptive, and indicative that a company's leaders have failed to take the kind of early preventive action that can avert the need for "transformation."

Nor does this mean that there is no place within Nestlé for fast change. In fact, Brabeck has an explicit ambition to accelerate the pace of change in the company. In his own words: "I had a general feeling that we were too slow. I said that this organization walks around in slippers. And although this is comfortable, it doesn't allow you to move fast. If you try, you fall on your face! So I said that we must move from slippers to tennis shoes and from tennis shoes to training shoes and from training shoes to running shoes. Where are we today? We are mostly in tennis shoes. We are starting to walk faster, but we need to be prepared to run."

The point, of course, is that the best pace varies according to requirements and context. Brabeck himself has not been afraid to act fast and radically when needed. Each member of the ten-strong executive board changed assignments or was retired the day Brabeck took over. During his tenure, Nestlé has put in place new global business structures in the pet food and water businesses; it has introduced a massive standardized information system project, Globe; and during 2002–2003, the company moved fast to make major acquisitions in pet food (Ralston Purina), frozen snacks (ChefAmerica), and ice cream (Dreyer's).

"Talking to my colleagues," says Brabeck, "I find half of them believe we're much too slow and the other half that we're much too fast . . . Clearly, we must be both. You have to accelerate where things are critical, and in other places you may need to go slow. The point is to find out what's critical. But there's no one answer."

Knowing the Score

Living with this level of complexity and ambiguity does not come easily to many. It presents distinctive leadership challenges. "Yesterday I took speed away from Globe at the center," Brabeck told us when we saw him recently. "I needed more resources in a critical pilot market. I have to win that battle first! So Globe will slow down a little—but nothing will collapse because of this delay—unlike if we fail in a pilot market! So it's slow down here, accelerate there! Some people are not comfortable with that level of ambiguity. But it seems to me you can't live in a black-and-white world any longer."

Brabeck has studied music and compares the challenges of leading a complex global business to those of musical orchestration. This implies a long and laborious period of preparation before the conductor is ready to conduct.

"The conductor works for a year before he goes to practice with the orchestra. When you look now at my first Nestlé blueprint, it is nothing spectacular. But I worked for eighteen months—thinking and talking and reading. Once you have the four pillars of the blueprint, it's simple and uncomplicated. You may say, why did it take all this time? But if you look at a complex company like ours and try to get the four issues which finally are the difference between failure and success, well, they are not just laying there—you have to find them. It's like a tune. It's so complex and so big. You must work through it—scrutinizing and questioning and talking and confronting. Finally, you see the line, like a composer—then it's so simple."

Brabeck is under no illusion about his central challenge as a leader: it is, in his words, to "excite others to follow him." But inheriting the leadership of a long-established giant company like Nestlé has parallels with the challenges facing a conductor inheriting another composer's work. The difficult part is to interpret the score in your own personal style: to be authentic rather than to imitate.

"The objective of the conductor is to show his interpretation of the soul of the work that someone else has composed. He needs to motivate others for that purpose—to make it his version . . . Like him, I want to get the maximum potentiality of this company. I want this to be an orchestra that has a sound which is unique. Just like the Vienna Philharmonic. No orchestra in the world has that sound. And here I want the most perfect sound that I can get."

Priority Juggling

Achieving this sound entails the constant balancing of priorities and pace—and the continuing management of ambiguity. Take three examples. First, even though Nestlé is a company where people, products, and brands are "untouchable" and always given preference before technology, there are, nevertheless, many examples of technological innovation and leadership. Nestlé led the establishment of virtual shopping, for example, through interactive television in advance of the Web. It was a pioneer in B2B commerce. It is currently implementing Globe—one of the most ambitious corporate data management and information systems projects in the world.

Second, the Nestlé *Leadership and Management Principles* carry enduring themes but have been recently rewritten to better reflect the new challenges facing Nestlé in the twenty-first century—and, in particular, the need for "continuous transformation." And third—perhaps as a result of its "unique sound"—this apparently plodding giant has actually become the fastest-growing business in the slow-growth food business.

Of course, not all leaders face the complex orchestration challenges of those who run global businesses. Nevertheless, questions of pace and timing are faced by all leaders. So are there guidelines that can help you to make the right calls as you communicate the need for change as a leader? Drawing on the work of our colleague John Hunt and our own consulting experience, we have found that effective leaders:[11]

Communicate sufficient pressure for change. For top business leaders, this is often a difficult call. While they personally are exposed to external pressures on a daily basis—financial analysts, aggressive acquisitors, regulators, the media, shareholders, and so on—many of their colleagues are not. Similarly, those at the edges of organizations—sales, servicing, procurement, advertising, and other customer- or supplier-facing jobs—are also more directly exposed to external pressure. But many internal functions and corporate jobs are less exposed, less uncomfortable, and, as a result, sometimes more complacent. So it is easy to exaggerate the extent to which people actually experience a sense of urgency even when it appears the pressures are obvious. Leaders often feel the need to push the pace before anyone has realized there is even a need to move. But racing ahead with initiatives before others—to use the jargon—have "unfrozen," is a common cause of failure for those who aspire to lead change.

Where there are strong external pressures, the communication challenge for leaders is to translate these into positive internal forces for change—without freezing people. The danger is that if there is too much pressure, people feel overwhelmed. In one high-tech company that we work with, a common complaint is that the CEO has consistently demanded that the existing business grow at double the rate of the market *and* that additional growth come from new business ventures. While people may respond positively to crisislike conditions—particularly if led well—*relentless* pressure can lead to burnout, exhaustion, and a fatalistic acceptance that "unrealistic" expectations will not be met.

In other cases, initiatives designed to install urgency may be greeted with a shrug as "yet another change program." Instead of kick-starting movement, they merely produce boredom, loss of energy, and cynicism.

Creating mechanisms for discomfort without alienating potential followers is a fine art that, in one way or another, we have touched upon in various parts of this book. It is often particularly challenging where the external pressures are actually not as strong as the leader might like. The organization is too comfortable. Think, for example, of the way in which Karel Vuursteen dramatically staged his visual presentation of the Anheuser-Busch shark jaws ready to swallow the apparently safe, family-owned Heineken fish. Or the skillful way in which Greg Dyke made his BBC colleagues (guaranteed a regular, large annual license-fee income) aware of the urgent need to reduce costs and cut jobs in some areas in order to resource their central purpose: making and broadcasting great programs. Finally, consider once more Peter Brabeck's gradual change of footwear for his colleagues in the relatively conservative and—in some markets, at least—comfortably placed giant Nestlé.

Communicate a clear and compelling vision. If a sense of pressure is the push, then a compelling vision is often the pull factor. An effective vision delivers an attractive picture of the future and draws people in to support its achievement. Leaders can generate a sense of excitement through their personal values and vision. But there are two key points in relation to pace and timing. First, an effective vision has staying power. It is memorable *over time.* Think of Microsoft's vision—"A computer on every desk in every home"—or BMW's "The ultimate driving experience." Too often, hastily constructed and ill-thought-out visions are almost instantly forgettable.

Second, no matter how vivid and emotionally exciting the vision, all the leaders we know report that actually communicating it takes longer than they expected. Success depends upon persistence, simple repeatable messages, and imaginative use of different channels. This is why stories can be so powerful: they are low-cost vehicles for attracting attention to the vision and engaging others in its elaboration and promulgation.

Signal where the capability challenge lies. If there is sufficient pressure and an attractive vision, it is worth considering next whether there is sufficient people capability to deliver. When we ask this question in our consulting work, it is remarkable how many people will quickly answer yes. But if you push for the evidence, it is typically thin. Organizations rarely seem to audit people resources in the same way they do financial or physical resources, for example.

In the absence of hard data, leaders who are in too much of a hurry tend to focus only on the people problems that look as if they can be fixed fast. Their apparent successes can be deceptive. Let us explain. The familiar matrix in figure 7-1 sees capability in terms of the two dimensions of performance and potential.

FIGURE 7-1

Assessing capability: performance and potential

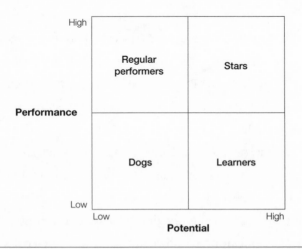

Where is it that leaders are most likely to look as if they have delivered a swift turnaround in capability? In our experience, it is in two boxes: the stars and the dogs. Here the issues can be dealt with relatively quickly and easily—if only because, in most organizations, their combined population is relatively small. Yet the more intractable problems, less amenable to quick fixes, typically lie in the other two categories, where the great majority of the population is actually located.

Think about it. The small group of elite stars—those with high current performance and future potential—are often provided with lavish fast-track development programs. Yet these are the very people who, almost by definition, are best able to look after themselves. And the dogs? Once they are identified, the issue is simple: managing their exit. How many organizations have been led down this quick-fix path and still failed to deliver performance? In many respects, some of the most spectacular collapses of companies in the 1990s were associated with "star" cultures that celebrated individual high achievers and ignored or exited regular performers who helped sustain the business day in and day out.[12]

In fact, it is in the careful and gradual nurturing of learners and the sustained celebration of regular performers that leaders are often able to achieve their greatest long-term impact. This is where the greater proportion of the organization population lies. The learners need time to grow and develop—and, of course, along the way some will fail. This requires the patience often associated with good gardening. In the world of sport, for example, the very best coaches are often exemplars of such careful husbandry.

With the regular performers, there is a familiar leadership challenge: to make them feel special. Too often, they are taken for granted or, even worse, denigrated as "plodders" or "solid citizens."

We know very few people who feel special when others label them as "solid." The irony, of course, is that the regular performers are the backbone of any organization, the people who keep the show on the road, the team that keeps you in business. And they are performing to the limits of their potential. What more can we expect? Shouldn't this be the aspiration for *everyone* in an organization?

The very best leaders understand this and are prepared to invest the time required to enable the learners to flourish and to celebrate the achievements of the regular performers. Remember the inclusive bias of leaders such as Greg Dyke, John Latham, and David Gardner, and the time and effort they are prepared to spend making *everyone* feel special. Recent research suggests that organizations that reproduce this kind of leader behavior are those that last longest.

Communicate actionable steps. We have worked with many organizations where the pressure for change is keenly felt, the vision is skillfully communicated, and there are highly capable people, but no one knows what to do first—or why. Nor do they understand how a first step might lead to another and so on until eventually the vision is achieved. In effect, there is a communication breakdown: no one can connect the grand vision to day-to-day actions. And until they can, all the talk of visions is just that: talk. A major communication task for leaders is to help people make connections between their daily work and the overarching purpose—to help them make sense of what they do.[13]

The classic case of the Komatsu-Caterpillar rivalry makes this point well. The story began in the 1960s. Komatsu, a local manufacturer of earthmoving equipment in downtown Tokyo, developed a grand vision: "Maru C" (Surround Caterpillar). At the time, Caterpillar appeared unassailable as the global leader in earthmoving machinery. The Komatsu vision appeared ambitious to say the least, but it was broken into actionable steps.

The first step was to improve quality and safety rather than to cut prices. No one wants to buy cheap but unsafe machinery. Once comparable quality standards were achieved, the next step was to reduce costs. Cheaper equipment of equal quality was—and is—a competitive proposition. After that came product differentiation and, finally, after-sales service. One step helped the achievement of the next, until the vision gradually became reality.

This is the logic that leaders must work hard to communicate, if they are to turn visions into concrete actions. And there are two—apparently paradoxical—imperatives in relation to pace and timing.

First, it is important to get started quickly. There is only so long before a vision without action will lose its credibility. Look before you leap is wise advice—but taken too far, it can produce analysis paralysis. As we often remind those we work with, "excellence is the enemy of the good." Good leaders get on and achieve quick wins that convince people that things might be changing. Remember the early interventions by John Latham and Greg Dyke to make the everyday working lives of their colleagues better. Their actions demonstrate a capability that Karl Weick has recently celebrated as the ability to "look while you leap."[14]

But just as it is important to get started *quickly*, it is equally necessary to realize that you will rarely get there in one leap. The second imperative is to divide change into sometimes *slower* steps—one at a time, with clear and gradual progression. Remember the imagery of Peter Brabeck's tennis shoes, training shoes, and running shoes.

Provide effective rewards for those who follow. Taking steps to change things can be risky, so those who follow should be rewarded. In effect, leaders must provide followers with an answer to the question "What's in it for me?" The danger is for the leader to assume that what they find rewarding is shared by followers. Rarely is life this simple.

Excitement will feel different for salespeople in comparison with research scientists. Recognition needs are met in quite distinctive ways for academics in comparison with actors. The community to which specialist lawyers aspire may be quite different from that of software engineers. And of course, individuals within all these occupational groups are unlikely to completely fit the stereotype. As we have seen in our examination of situation sensing, effective leaders recognize these differences and build a rich picture of those they lead.

In addition, they understand that what gets measured gets done—and here we return once more to the vital issue of pace. Too often, achievement of short-term, clearly measurable targets can distract attention from more important longer-term objectives

At PolyGram, CEO Alain Levy clearly understood the difference. While one country business clearly exceeded its annual sales targets by reissuing existing material and ignoring the nurturing of new talent, another persistently missed annual targets as it sought to launch new acts and develop the repertoire. After three years of apparent failure, patience paid off in year four. A new act was discovered, launched, and successfully promoted on a wider scale. The revenue stream that followed far outstripped the incremental achievement of the other country business. Levy rewarded the team handsomely—and let it be known that he had. Needless to say, the episode quickly became a PolyGram "story," neatly illustrating the kind of long-term, creative behaviors that produced the biggest rewards.

Balancing short-term requirements with longer-term strategic objectives and visionary aspirations is a familiar dilemma replayed across many settings and all levels. Leaders everywhere need to consider pressure for change, vision, capability, getting started, and targeted rewards. Hospitals must balance waiting-list targets with broader aspirations to treat illness more effectively. Schools need to balance grade achievements in exams with the social well-being and self-esteem of pupils. Pharmaceutical companies must trade short-term market share against longer-term commitments for breakthrough cures. These are issues not just for those at the strategic apex but for nurses, teachers, and researchers all over the organization.

Set against these competing demands, reward systems are never perfect. The best that leaders can achieve is an arrangement that flexes fast as the market changes and priorities shift. But to repeat, fast adaptation should not be at the expense of longer-term aspirations or, indeed, basic ethical considerations. This theme is the focus of the concluding chapter. But before we reach that point, we must look at the world more fully through the eyes of the follower. For even though we have stressed that effective leadership relies on the skills of managing social distance, communicating with impact, and understanding pace, timing, and orchestration, none of this will work unless it connects with the followers.

Authentic Followership

FOLLOWERS ARE THE OTHER SIDE of the leadership equation. Without them, there is no relationship and no leadership. If leadership is a dynamic relationship, and the appropriate balance of closeness and distance keeps changing to fit new circumstances, it is logical that followers, too, live in the same dynamic relationship, but see things from a different perspective.

If the leaders get the balance right, followers feel comfortable. They are glad to be close to their leader; they feel that their individuality is recognized and that they are part of a team. The leader has shown enough of himself that the followers know he is not perfect, and that has two results. First, it gives them permission to be less than perfect as well. Second, it tells them that the leader needs the contribution they can make to the team.

At the same time, the leader's distance shows the follower that this person is not afraid to make tough decisions and be unpopular. Among the many leaders we have met and interviewed is Brigadier Pat Lawless. On graduating from the Rhodesian Army's officer training school, he chose to lead one of the most important black regiments in the country's civil war. He told us that when he first took up his post, he was heavily reliant on his black second in command. On his first visit to the sergeants' mess, he told Lawless in no uncertain terms that to be an effective leader, he should not expect—or even seek—to be universally popular. Sure, he wanted most people to like him, but what mattered was that even those who didn't like him had to respect him. For Lawless, and for us, it was an important lesson in leadership. The leader must always be seen as serving the organization's higher purpose or goal, not swayed by personal considerations.

There are pitfalls for followers, too. As with leaders, they must understand the limits to closeness and the difference between closeness and friendship. They must sense that when the leader adds distance, he or she is acting in service to the organization's cause rather than turning on them. Without that understanding, followers are apt to feel too special and star-struck when the balance shifts toward closeness, or betrayed and resentful when the leader shows distance. Remember, however close the leader gets, this is a person who might one day have to fire you.

A leader who abuses either distance or closeness will be seen as devious and manipulative. Followers in that case need no advice. They will shut down emotionally to minimize the damage to them, and they will probably start looking for other jobs. In the long run, that kind of bad leadership tends to be self-correcting. The sort of cynical, indifferent employees they foster are unlikely to do good work. Sooner or later, the leader will be held accountable and replaced. Unfortunately, this can take a long time—and a great deal of damage can be done to the organization in the interim.

When the leader does get the balance right, however, it is a positive situation for everyone. Both leader and followers have the heady feeling of working as a well-honed team for the organization's overriding cause or goal. Since people who feel that way are more likely to succeed, that's good for the organization, its customers and partners, and its investors. And that's both the reward and the definition of good leadership.

What Do Followers Want?

So, put yourself in the role of follower and ask, What do you expect of a leader?

Surprisingly, perhaps, researchers seldom ask the question explicitly. We have libraries full of leadership studies, but the analysis of followership has barely begun.[1] Yet it is difficult to operate effectively as a leader without some sense of what followers want or need.

In chapters 4 and 5, we argued that effective leaders are sensitive to context—including the requirements of their followers—and are able flex their style accordingly. But is it possible to generalize about what followers want? In the course of our work, we have asked many followers, and their replies included many different things. But we still conclude that their responses are patterned and can be described under four broad headings. The four elements followers want from leaders are authenticity, significance, excitement, and community.

Further, despite the paucity of dedicated followership research, there is a large body of organizational analysis that, when unpacked, supports our observations. This is the ever-expanding research on motivation, team behavior, and communication. What's more, our personal experience of working firsthand with leaders is that the best of them intuitively grasp these universal principles and act on them.

Authenticity

First, and above all, followers demand authenticity. We want our leaders to show us who they are—to reveal some of their real human differences. Leaders who lack this authenticity have a fatal flaw. So, even though it is a struggle to define it, we know inauthenticity when we see it.

Every follower will answer the question "Why should I be led by you?" by considering what's *different* about you (that might be attractive to me as a follower)? Your skill at displaying these personal differences represents the foundation for your leadership. The best examples of leaders in this book excel in their followers' eyes by being themselves. They know themselves and show themselves—skillfully.

As we noted, carefully communicating "who you are" often relies upon choosing the channels that work for you. Think back to Thomas Sattelberger's careful staging of his town meetings or Simon Gulliford's road shows.

So now ask yourself, Are you clear about the differences that work for you in a leadership context? Do you communicate these skillfully to others? Do they know something of who you are and where you come from?

Significance

Second, followers need to feel significant. In simple terms, they need recognition for their contribution. Social psychologists have made repeated pronouncements on this profound human need for recognition. So it is remarkable how often as individuals we seem to want it but not give it. The result is a recognition deficit. Why is this? There are many explanations. Some executives just seem to be too busy. It simply doesn't come high enough in their day-to-day priorities. They mistake activity for effectiveness.[2] These are the people who save up their recognition—good and bad—for the annual appraisal.

Others seem temperamentally unsuited to giving the kind of personalized feedback that is essential to skillful recognition. Don't forget the disproportionate number of introverts who find their way into leadership roles at the top of hierarchies. Of course, introverts can make others feel important—but it tends to take a lot more effort. In yet other cases, the problems appear to be cultural. The British, for example, are often uncomfortable both giving and receiving praise. There are also some particularly aggressive corporate cultures where the imperative is to "just do it." Recognition is for wimps.

All our experience is that effective leaders find ways to break through these barriers. Martin Sorrell may be a tough, finance-driven leader, but it does not prevent him from taking the time to carefully, swiftly, and personally respond to e-mails from colleagues around the world. Greg Dyke openly praised the contributions of individuals all over the reserved and very "British" BBC within days of taking up his post. Think also of John Latham finding time to write the note to his harassed colleague at the end of a difficult day in the classroom: "You are marvelous."

During his long tenure as CEO and chairman of GE, Jack Welch was well known for his handwritten notes. He might thank a colleague for a job well done, or simply encourage them to greater efforts. But the point is that despite his colossal workload, Welch made the time to jot down a few well-chosen words of recognition.

He knew how important it was. The great thing about a handwritten note, of course, is that it is both highly personalized and lasting. A colleague of ours was recently visiting an eminent Japanese business consultant and thinker in Tokyo and noticed he had a note from Welch framed on his wall. Many GE employees have similar testaments to their leader's recognition.

Or think of Thomas Sattelberger's careful use of his eyes to ensure that everyone at his meetings felt he was looking at *them*. Finally, remember Pete Goss's aim to make all his crew members feel that the voyage could not have been completed without *their* personal involvement. As you consider these cases, ask yourself these questions: Do you pay the same kind of attention to those that you wish to lead? Do you make them feel that what they are trying to achieve is important, and that they themselves have a vital role to play?

Excitement

Third, followers need a sense of excitement. At root, leadership involves exciting others to higher levels of effort and performance. It is more than simply getting things done or carrying on doing today what we did yesterday. How do leaders lift people in this way? How do they communicate this excitement? Partly it is through using their personal differences. Partly it is through the movement from personal closeness to distance and the sense of edge that this often creates. Some of the most effective leaders we have seen retain a rather enigmatic quality as a result of their management of social distance. This, in turn, can make them a little mysterious and, yes, exciting.

But beyond this, leaders are often able to excite others through their passionate commitment to clearly articulated personal values and to a vision. This is a well-worked theme in the leadership literature. Business leaders such as Steve Jobs, Bill Gates, Jack Welch, and Anita Roddick seem able to infect others with their passions, whatever they may be. Effective leaders produce electrifying moments.

Sometimes when we have finished leadership development workshops, we ask participants two questions that often produce perplexed looks. First, do you excite people to higher performance every day that you are at work? Second, how will people feel when you return to your workplace after this workshop? Will they say, "Great, she's back, brimming with new thoughts," or will they be worrying about just what you will be complaining about this time? Are you a source of energy in your organization? Or a drain? Asking these questions can produce interesting and sometimes disturbing insights.

Community

Fourth, followers want to feel part of a community. Human beings are hardwired for sociability—and desire solidarity. They have a deep-rooted desire to belong, to feel part of something bigger, to relate to others—not just the leader. The nature of the wider community varies. Some are intense and all-encompassing, others more diverse and fragmented, as we outlined in chapter 5. But however it is expressed, there is a basic desire to relate that effective leaders tap into. Remember David Gardner's celebratory trip, taking the entire European EA workforce to the French holiday resort?

Or think of head teacher John Latham's personal crusade against litter, a graphic reminder of the rights and responsibilities of *all* school community members. Finally, consider Paul McDermott's long-term loyalty to the troubled community that he has served for almost twenty years.

So ask yourself, Do you engender a sense of belonging? Are you a community builder? Do you help people to connect—to each other and to the overarching purpose of the organization?

When individuals communicate their own authenticity and generate a sense of significance, excitement, and community to others, they are getting the basics of the leadership relationship right. They are helping their followers to answer constructively these fundamental questions: Why are we here? What is our purpose? What can we achieve together? Why are you the leader?

What Makes a Follower?

If these four elements are what followers expect of their leaders, what, in turn, should leaders expect of followers? What is it that makes a good follower? And how can followers contribute to the creation of effective and authentic leadership? Ultimately, these are questions for all of us since although *some* may become leaders, we are *all* followers.

What makes these questions pressing is the persisting evidence that followers are often able to "lead" leaders astray. In the early 1960s, for example, President Kennedy escalated the U.S. intervention in Vietnam on the basis of, at best, questionable intelligence and advice from colleagues. Some forty years later, Prime Minister Tony Blair's support for the Iraq invasion appeared to be on the basis of similarly fallible inputs from advisers. In a business context, remember also how Ken Lay, the Enron chairman, blamed unscrupulous subordinates for his company's dramatic fall from grace. In each of these cases, detractors will argue that the leaders heard what they wanted to hear. But like leading, following is a two-way street.

Research by Lynn Offerman shows that leaders may fall victim to followers in a number of different ways.[3] First, there are followers who impose a version of majority rule. Classically, for example, technology-led companies—dominated by technologists—often develop products that appeal greatly to their technical colleagues but mean very little to end consumers. At different times, IBM, Apple, and Dell, for instance, have all experienced large-scale failures at least partially explained by leaders unable to resist the unerring logic of the collective ranks of their technical specialists.

Second, there are circumstances where leaders may be fooled by a subtler manipulation: flattery. We like those who like us. But leaders—especially those with narcissistic tendencies—are prone to swallowing wholesale the adulation of others and to developing an exaggerated sense of self-worth. This is one way of explaining how senior executives, sometimes with exemplary leadership track records, may damage their hard-won reputations by accepting lavish compensation or retirement deals toward the end of their careers.

In each of these cases, followers may play an active—although not always conscious or intentional—part in the derailment of leaders. But clearly, there are also circumstances where potential followers are simply disengaged or alienated from aspiring leaders and their organizations. In many respects, this detachment may be the most worrying symptom of modern organizational life. Just as bureaucratic roles squeeze out the lifeblood of leadership, so too they create disengaged subordinates rather than actively engaged followers.

Throughout this book, we have argued that effective leaders are able to excite and engage followers. But we have also maintained that leadership is a (nonhierarchical) relationship. Subordinates may not decide who their bosses are, but it is the followers who ultimately decide who the leaders are. By definition, then, "good followers" are actively engaged. They are volunteers, not conscripts—and, not surprisingly, they share some of the characteristics of good leaders. In a modern organization, many leaders must at times occupy followers' positions. Indeed, Aristotle once noted that all great leaders must first learn to follow. So what makes a good follower?

First, they are prepared to speak up—even if this involves significant personal risks. Good followers will tell leaders what they see as the truth—whether they want to hear it or not. Warren Bennis quotes the legendary movie mogul Sam Goldwyn, who, following a series of box office disasters, brought his staff together and told them, "I want you to tell me exactly what's wrong with me and MGM, even if it means losing your job."[4]

What is it that motivates followers to endure these risks? Ultimately—as with leaders—it has to do with the fact that they too share some commitment to an overarching purpose. At their best, conscientious followers will try to remind leaders "why we are here." They care enough about the organization, its mission, and their own linked ambitions to be able to voice concerns and criticisms. In extreme cases, and as a last resort, this takes the form of whistle blowing. But it is much healthier when followers who are prepared to confront their leaders are listened to and addressed.

Of course, not all followers will voice the same concerns. Indeed, if good leaders look for diversity and constructive dissent, we should expect those who speak up to be different. Remember Peter Brabeck's remark that half his colleagues felt things were changing too fast; the other half felt the pace was too slow? The job of the leader is typically to hear these different voices and to then search for a common focus or set of interests that can form the basis of their leadership.

Second, followers are prepared to complement the leader. They develop a sense of what is required of them in different situations. They recognize the importance of smooth interpersonal skills in what we termed networked cultures, for example. By contrast, they will appreciate that mercenary cultures place a higher premium on disciplined, swift action. They understand the importance of freedom, autonomy, and only limited interaction in fragmented cultures. But those in tightly knit communal cultures actively seek out the intense, collective interactions that typically hold such organizations together.

Within the team, they will provide a counterweight. We pointed earlier to the apparently intuitive ability of some leaders to achieve balance. This starts typically with an awareness of their own strengths and shortcomings—and an ability to spot those who can help them. But good followers will often repay the compliment—knowing well what the leader can and cannot do, understanding weaknesses and reacting accordingly. You will often see this kind of teamwork in business in the relationship between an effective chairman and chief executive; or in sports, between manager and coach. Like the best leaders, good followers understand what they do best and when. They are able to be themselves—more.

Third, followers have a skillful appreciation of change and timing. They understand that leaders must conform—up to a point. Without this, leaders are unlikely to find points of connection or common cause with those they would like as followers. But once followers see evidence of both competence and conformity—that leaders can do what they say and are loyal—they are likely to grant leaders scope for innovation and change. E. P. Hollander calls this "idiosyncrasy credit."[5]

Political leaders with narrow majorities often build up such credits, as President Clinton did to win support for his programs during his first administration. Similarly, Tony Blair was granted opportunities to create "new" Labour once party members were convinced of his abilities to protect at least some of the crown jewels of "old" Labour (social welfare, the National Health Service, and so on). In each case, apparently reluctant followers are more party to the change process than is often acknowledged.

But just as followers can sanction change as well as continuity, they are also able to tolerate leaders shifting between social closeness and distance. They do not confuse leaders with their best friends. Rather, they recognize the moment when separation, if only temporary, is necessary and even inevitable to achieve the shared purpose.

Skillful followership, then, inevitably involves acceptance of some degree of ambiguity and uncertainty. This runs against popular wisdom, which holds that followers look to leaders to provide security particularly during times of uncertainty. Followers who expect the leader to have all the answers are naïve—and such expectations do their leaders no favors. The point, in an increasingly fast-changing and complex world, is to help leaders to learn. Followers should encourage a process of mutual exploration as both parties cope with changing contexts and demands.

In the process, some followers may become leaders. The reverse will certainly apply: there are always places where leaders will need to follow. Ultimately, the followers' duty is to resist blind obedience and to know when to withdraw support from the failing leader. This can be a fine line. Leadership, as we have said through-

NINE

The Price and Prize
of Leadership

IN THIS BOOK, we have tried to help you address a difficult and challenging question: Why should anyone be led by you? There aren't easy answers to this question. Leadership is complicated—and the secrets of great leadership resist simple recipes. Successful leaders who share their insight and experience in published autobiographies give us important clues—but cannot provide "the answer." And those aspiring leaders who attempt to mimic their heroes make a fatal error. The point is to be more like yourself, not more like someone else. No one can write this particular recipe other than you. As with this book, we doubt you'll write it overnight. To be yourself more with skill is a lifelong task.

Look beyond the autobiographies to the leadership research for an answer to our question, and you may also be disappointed. Too much of it has focused on individuals, neglecting the reality that leadership is a relationship. What's more, these individuals are often men at or near the top of hierarchies. As we have pointed out, confusing hierarchy and leadership has been a fatal flaw undermining many discussions of leadership. Hierarchy can help you if you are a leader—but it can never explain your leadership.

"Scientific" attempts to measure the patterned differences of individuals who have acted as leaders have largely failed. The definitive list of leadership attributes has never been completed— because there isn't one. If there were, it would need to be constantly changed as contexts shifted and relationships changed. In effect, this explains why new recipes are appearing year in, year out. The recent fashion for so-called quiet leaders, rather than the larger-than-life charismatic heroes celebrated during the 1990s, is yet another illustration of how style must fit context and era. As times change, so do our expectations of leaders.

Beyond Easy Answers

We have tried to resist a recipe—and we have included in our book men and women in very different places, all over organizations. Our central contention, then, is that leadership is *situational, nonhierarchical, and relational.* You might feel this is almost common sense—but you would be surprised how often it is forgotten.

What's required of leaders will inevitably be shaped by context and relationships. A primary skill must be to sense these different contexts: to understand time and place and to respond accordingly.

Effective leaders know the limits to their actions as well as the opportunities; when to get close to others and when to separate; when to accelerate and when to slow down. Effective leaders cannot be properly explained by a list of desirable attributes. Their success stems from active engagement in a complex series of relationships carefully cultivated—often in contrasting contexts.

Those who get this right survive in order to fulfill their purpose. Those who get it wrong are often derailed. The high rates of CEO turnover that have attracted interest over recent years, for example, can be at least partially be explained, in our terms, by poor situation sensing and an inability to connect with those these executives aspire to lead. But media attention on the failures of high-profile leaders should not lead us to the conclusion that these challenges are unique to senior executives. Such individuals attract our attention because they are high-profile figures in big jobs. We know something of them, and feel we can make a judgment.

But the same challenges face all leaders all over organizations. For leadership is nonhierarchical—and great organizations have leaders at many levels. We have introduced you to some of these lesser-known leaders in the pages of this book. Wherever they are, their challenges are identical: to be themselves—but skillfully and in context. For it is the person we follow, not the position. The best of these individuals show enough of their authentic selves—their differences, passions, values, and even weaknesses—to engage and excite their followers. Arguably, their authenticity has never been in greater demand.

The Leader Undone

We have referred to many leaders in this book—from senior executives in large commercial enterprises to individuals relatively low down the hierarchy in voluntary organizations. You may have noticed that some are no longer in their jobs. We cannot let this pass. We must discuss the processes through which the leader is undone.

Perhaps the most spectacular case is the demise of Greg Dyke as director general of the BBC. As he puts it himself in his perceptive autobiography, Dyke went "from the most powerful media job in the UK to unemployed in just three days."[1] The man who had made a bigger difference to the BBC than perhaps any leader in the last fifty years was forced to resign by his own board of governors. Indeed, the stark choice was resign or be sacked. So what precipitated this dramatic reversal of Dyke's fortunes?

First, the bare bones of the story. On May 29, 2003, a report by BBC journalist Andrew Gilligan on the *Today* program, the BBC's flagship radio news show, accused the U.K. government and in particular those close to Tony Blair, of "sexing up" the report of Saddam Hussein's alleged weapons of mass destruction in Iraq. This was the trigger for a confrontation between the BBC and the British government, which would cost the corporation both its chairman, the former Goldman Sachs economist Gavyn Davis, and its CEO, Greg Dyke. It culminated in the publication of the Hutton Report, Lord Hutton's inquiry into the events surrounding the dispute, including the tragic suicide of Dr. David Kelly, a senior weapons expert at the heart of the argument. The Hutton Report almost completely exonerated the government and laid the blame for the mess wholly at the door of the BBC. Dyke was forced to stand down.

His resignation produced an extraordinary response from the employees—not famed for either their general happiness or their love of management. Thousands poured onto the streets, not only in London, but in large regional centers and in the national capitals of Wales, Scotland, and Northern Ireland. Herb Schlosser, former president and CEO of NBC, remarked, "I saw on the Internet BBC employees marching in support of a CEO. This is the first in the history of the Western world."[2] Part of this was stimulated by Greg Dyke's own leaving e-mail, which we reproduce here in full. It is evidence of his strong emotional and intellectual connection to the BBC as an institution and to its people.

This is the hardest e-mail I've ever written. In a few moments, I'll be announcing to the outside world that I'm leaving after four years as Director General. I don't want to go and I'll miss everyone here hugely. However, the management of the BBC was heavily criticized in the Hutton Report and as Director General I am responsible for the management.

I accept that the BBC made errors of judgement and I've sadly come to the conclusion that it will be hard to draw a line under this whole affair while I am still here. We need closure. We need closure to protect the future of the BBC, not for you or for me but for the benefit of everyone out there. It might sound pompous but I believe the BBC really matters. Throughout this affair my sole aim as Director General of the BBC has been to defend our editorial independence and to act in the public interest.

In four years, we've achieved a lot between us. I believe we've changed the place fundamentally and I hope those changes will last beyond me. The BBC has always been a great organization but I hope that, over the last four years, I've helped to make it a more human place where everyone who works here feels appreciated. If that's anywhere near true I leave contented if sad.

Thank you all for the help and support you've given me. This might sound schmaltzy but I really will miss you all.

Greg.[3]

Follower Activism

More than six thousand employees responded to Dyke's e-mail—the overwhelming majority regretting the demise of their leader. In his account of the events, Dyke picks out two in particular. They provide eloquent testimony to the impact he had upon the organization.

Your greatest achievement was giving the kiss of life to a body of people who'd been systematically throttled, castrated, and lobotomized. To leave us very much alive and kicking, loving the BBC and respecting the role of Director General again, is a fantastic legacy.[4]

. . . pay testimony to the vision and energy you have brought to the BBC. Men and women, even journalists, cried today. People came together and talked about their emotions, their fears, their frustrations all because the man who had embodied the hope, the vision, the pride they had begun to feel about the future of the organization had gone.[5]

All the evidence, including hard data on staff morale, shows that Dyke made a huge impact on this difficult organization. How can it have happened that he was forced into an unhappy resignation?

Let us be clear. Our view is that his forced departure was extremely damaging to the organization. He was and is an inspirational leader, and, as we have tried to show in this book, there are things that all who aspire to leadership can learn from his experience. But there are lessons too in his demise. Dyke unquestionably made mistakes.

A continuing theme in our argument is that effective leadership absolutely depends on the expression of authentic self. The simple maxim is "Be yourself." On this Dyke scored well. He is curious about himself—that is to say, he pursues self-knowledge (up to a point) and is quite prepared to disclose what he really cares about. As we discussed earlier, he also reveals weakness— occasional temper outbursts, for example. But there is something more—a fatal flaw, perhaps. There is something of a pattern to his career. Dyke left the television company TV-AM after one year, when he fell out badly with his Australian boss, Bruce Gyngell. He subsequently lost the battle to retain control of his beloved London Weekend Television (LWT), beginning a feud with fund manager Mercury Asset Management that still rankles. And finally, he lost the biggest job in U.K. media and one of the most important broadcasting jobs in the world. The truth is, Greg loves a fight, and he finds it very difficult to walk away from one. He acknowledges this himself at many points in his autobiography. For example, on the BBC's response to the Hutton Report, he says, "On BBC News 24 it was immediately interpreted as 'a robust response' from the BBC. Personally, I thought it was conciliatory, but then being conciliatory is not necessarily one of my stronger points so perhaps I wasn't the best person to judge."[6]

When LWT was acquired by Granada Television after a bitter struggle, Dyke was invited to stay. He declined. He saw the new owners as "the enemy." For him, perhaps, the world is divided into friends and enemies a little too clearly.

We have also suggested that effective leadership requires high levels of situation sensing. Again, Dyke was excellent at identifying the low levels of morale among program makers at the BBC. He had, and has, strong empathy with the talented, creative people who make organizations like the BBC really fly. In addition, he identifies with people lower down the hierarchy—the catering staff, the security people, and the drivers—many of whom were among his greatest admirers. But what of his situation sensing among the Establishment figures who came to dominate the BBC's board of governors?

As we noted earlier, initially Dyke tried to get on with them. But at the very core of his being, he could not pretend to respect people he did not. It was a political game he refused to play. "I saw no reason why I should treat the governors any differently from the way I treated everyone else. I certainly wasn't going to regard the earth they walked on as if it was somehow holy ground. This wasn't a wilful decision. It was just the way I am."[7]

This was his undoing. In particular, Dyke underestimated the opposition of the governors he called the "posh ladies": Baroness Hogg and Dame Pauline Neville-Jones. He knew they didn't like him, but believed at the height of the furor surrounding the Hutton Report that he had a deal with Dame Pauline, a longtime governor and former senior civil servant with strong links to the government machine, that he would stay. She had other ideas. Baroness Hogg also undermined Dyke's position by launching an attack on all he stood for. When they delivered the news that he must resign or be sacked, he was taken completely by surprise. "Of course I should have seen it coming," he later acknowledged, "but I hadn't. I was completely shocked."[8]

Judgment Calls

We have also argued in this book that effective leaders identify with those they lead. Again, Greg Dyke measures up well on this

ally in pursuit of a goal. They cannot avoid the ethical imperative that choosing a goal entails. This explains why Max Weber was so convinced that charismatic leadership was the best defense against the endless bureaucratization of the world—or as he memorably put it, "the disenchantment of the world." It is the necessity of the ethical imperative that prevents the subjugation of human life merely to technical rationality. Technical rationality says that whatever your problem, we can find a technically rational solution to it. The ethical imperative is the *why* that precedes the wherefore; it provides the meaning.

But even Weber had to concede that leadership can also be dangerous. There is no guarantee that effective leaders will achieve "good." Indeed, human history is littered with leaders whose capacity to excite others has led to almost unfathomable harm. Many of the greatest crimes against humanity can be laid at the door of charismatic leaders. Without an ethical purpose, leadership is simply an instrument for bending the efforts of the many to the will of one.

However, we remain optimistic. Our view is that effective leadership can have such a profound effect on the pursuit of noble goals that we must not flinch from it. We cannot let the dangers of leadership deflect us from exploring the many ways in which individuals can become more effective leaders in their own contexts. It is precisely because leadership can be so powerful in releasing human energies that leaders must ask and answer tough ethical questions.

For business enterprises, these are questions about purpose: what are corporations really for? For the capitalist enterprise, the answer has traditionally been to increase shareholder value. Indeed, passionate advocates of this view, such as the economist Milton Friedman, have argued that this is the only morally defensible position, and that any other involves mere employees—CEOs and other executives—imposing their personal values on organizations they do not own. In our view, notions such as shareholder value alone are inadequate as a basis for leadership. On the contrary, successful enterprises in the long term are energized in pursuit of some other goal, and it is as a by-product of this that they deliver value to shareholders.

In all the time we have spent in and around organizations, we have never heard a phone call that began, "Sorry, I'll be home late tonight—I'm increasing shareholder value." We have heard calls about helping colleagues, delighting customers, making great music, pushing on with research, getting personally rich—all manner of things—but never has the mantra of shareholder value moved anyone to exceptional performance.

This may help to explain the contemporary obsession with corporate governance—a procedural attempt to answer a moral question. Leaders cannot hide here, either. Whether they like it or not, the goals they set have ethical consequences. They may find inspiration in the words of David Hume, that most passionate of rationalists. "Avarice, or the desire of gain," he notes, "is a universal passion, which operates at all times, at all places, and upon all persons."[9] It's curious that an eighteenth-century Scottish philosopher comes so close to expressing the prevailing spirit of the modern age.

Yet, in these troubled times, we favor the view of another giant of the Enlightenment: Immanuel Kant. His ethical theories are most clearly expressed in his doctrine of autonomy, which has huge significance for many of the key themes of this book.

First, he insists, we can never rely on hierarchy as the basis of morality—whenever we are faced with a command, we have a duty to judge its morality. This is as relevant to the shredders of Enron documents as to the U.S. prison guards at Abu Ghraib. It relates directly to our insistence that leadership is nonhierarchical and relational, and it highlights the ethical responsibilities that fall to both leaders and followers.

Second, Kant tries to suggest a principle that could guide our conscience—this also seems of burning relevance to the world we live in now: "Always regard every man as an end in himself, and never use him merely as a means to your ends."[10] This inspirational moral principle addresses precisely the concerns with which we began this book—the necessity of shared moral values as a condition of our freedoms, and the search for a sense of community in an age where the old sources of social integration are getting weaker. Leaders and their followers can work together to create organizations that are sources of meaning, communities in which individuals can build and express their authentic selves.

For leaders, this will always involve personal risk. They must always be willing to commit themselves—knowing that they can be undone. This is the price and prize of leadership.

Charles de Gaulle poignantly observed of those who aspired to lead, "The price they have to pay for leadership is unceasing self-discipline, the constant taking of risks, and perpetual inner struggle . . . whence that vague sense of melancholy which hangs about the skirts of majesty."[11]

Leadership with Purpose

Leadership is hard, but worth it. So don't let us end on a pessimistic note. We are constantly and pleasantly surprised by the ways in which leaders in a myriad of settings bring meaning and high performance to organizations. They provide purpose and excitement; they live on the edge between uniqueness and a necessary degree of conformity. They make a difference.

Just as we were finishing this book, we were lucky enough to attend the retirement party of the senior partner in a local community medical practice. The doctor was well known locally for his charity and community work as well as for his professional accomplishments. The hall was packed with hundreds of his patients, each of whom was greeted personally by the doctor on arrival at the event. This created a lengthy queue, but no one seemed to mind. Then came the speeches. From patients, colleagues, and friends alike, a consistent story emerged:

"You are irreplaceable."

"You are Dr. John, you weren't just playing out a role."

"You treated each of us as individuals—not a number."

"You were never off duty."

"You really cared."

"You helped us build a great practice."

"You showed your passion—for charity fund-raising, for the local council—and for fast cars."

"You never stopped working—thank God you had a supportive wife."

"On the charity treks—even when surrounded by people twenty years younger, you were always at the front!"

Toward the end of the party, a fellow charity trekker spoke movingly of the occasion that Dr. John interrupted a hike to spend the best part of two days making himself available to locals in need of medical attention in a remote location in the Himalayas.

"It's wonderful, what you have said," confessed a clearly moved Dr. John at the close, "but as many of you know, I can be a really awkward customer to work with when I want."

The event was a poignant reminder—leadership emerges in all kinds of places. Dr. John was a person more than a role player. He made his patients feel special through the exercise of skill. He revealed his passions, including fast cars. He helped build a great practice. He knew that leadership was not a part-time job. And finally, in his closing remarks, he recognized insightfully that his care for the task could sometimes make him difficult to work with. So much about him connects to the abiding themes of this book. He was himself, he communicated his differences, but with skill, and in context. His colleagues and patients were happy—proud, even—to be led by him.

Now ask yourself the question: *Why should anyone be led by you?*

Evaluating Your
Leadership Potential

A S WE HAVE DEVELOPED our ideas, we have, of course, applied them with many who aspire to leadership in a variety of contexts. These include businesses, military organizations, churches, charities, sports teams, and government. In all these contexts, the same fundamental questions recur.

In what follows, you will not find a neat recipe for leadership. If there were one, someone would have found it by now. Neither do we wish to imply that developing as a leader is easy. It isn't. We are constantly impressed by how hard effective leaders work at their craft.

Nevertheless, we have found that asking individuals to consider these questions, calmly and reflectively, can really help them focus on their leadership potential and how it might be developed.

But don't expect the answers to be easy. Let us tell you about the first time we used this list of questions. We were working with a group of accomplished executives and had discussed with them our ideas about leadership. We nervously gave them the following questions to think about. Within half an hour, we discovered one of them lying on a sofa, apparently asleep. It looked as if the questions did not work! As we passed him, he opened his eyes, and we apprehensively asked, "How's it going?" "These are the hardest questions anyone has ever asked me," he replied. So try them yourself.

1. **Which personal differences could form the basis of your leadership capability?** As you think this through, focus on differences that have the potential to excite others, are genuinely yours (not copies of someone else's), and signify something important in your context. Think, too, about your personal values and vision for those you are leading. (See chapter 2.)

2. **Which personal weaknesses do you reveal to those you are leading?** Remember, it's a trap to pretend that you are perfect! But on the other hand, your leadership is unlikely to be enhanced by the revelation of *all* your weaknesses. Nor are those around you likely to be impressed by fallibilities that vitally undermine your performance. Effective leaders are able to focus others' dissatisfaction around personal foibles that, paradoxically, make them more human and so more attractive. (See chapter 3.)

3. **Are you able to read different contexts?** This starts with your ability to pick up and interpret soft data. Think hard about how well you are able to pick up on subtle shifts in the behavior of others. Are you equally adept with bosses,

peers, and subordinates? With customers and competitors? With those you like as well as those you dislike? How do you adapt across cultures? Are you better one-to-one, in a small group, or with large gatherings? (See chapter 4.)

4. **Do you conform enough?** Remember, you are unlikely to survive for long if you cannot recognize the moment to hold back; nor will you connect with others if you cannot find common ground. Think through your ability to gain acceptance with others—without losing your authenticity. (See chapter 5.)

5. **How well do you manage social distance?** Are you able to get close to those you lead? Do you know the goals, values, and motives of those who have the biggest impact on your performance? What do you need to know more about? Are you able to separate and create distance from others—at the right moment? What is your default mode: closeness or distance? (See chapter 6.)

6. **Do you have a good sense of organizational time?** Do you know when to speed up and when to take more time? Are you able to skillfully orchestrate the efforts of others? (See chapter 7.)

7. **How well do you communicate?** You can think about this in many ways. For example, how well do you communicate your personal differences, your weaknesses, your values and vision? Are you better in formal or informal contexts? Can you personalize your communications—through humor, example, and stories? How good are you at listening? Can you adapt to the different needs of different followers? (See chapters 7 and 8.)

Maximizing Authenticity and Skill

A N ABIDING THEME OF THIS BOOK is that effective leadership is about both authenticity and skill. We have observed some aspiring leaders who never quite manage this combination. Consider the simple matrix in figure B-1; think about where you are now, where you want to get to, and what you need to work on to be there.

In box B, skill and authenticity combine to produce leadership.

In box A, individuals have a strong sense of who they are, what made them, and what they stand for. But they lack the skills to deploy their attributes. They may fail to read contexts, to communicate well, and to see the world through the eyes of potential followers.

Balancing authenticity and skill

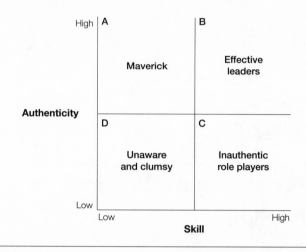

In box C, we find individuals with considerable interpersonal skills but whose lack of groundedness means that followers often feel that they are being worked—manipulated and sometimes exploited. They never display enough humanity to become really effective leaders.

In box D, low levels of both self-awareness and skill combine to produce a David Brent character so effectively satirized in the TV series *The Office*—and sadly prevalent in some organizations.

In the most abstract terms, movement along the skills axis is rather easier than increasing authenticity. Much standard business-school fare is concerned with the former; the latter takes longer and requires deeper interventions.

ACKNOWLEDGMENTS

A great many people have helped us in our quest to learn more about the nature of leadership. Over the last five years, we have talked to hundreds of leaders at all levels in organizations. In most places in the book, we identify those we talked with, but in some cases, we have altered names and some personal details in order to protect confidentiality. We owe a huge debt to all of those who took the time to answer our questions and to share their experiences and insights.

Particular thanks are due to Norman Adami, Dawn Austwick, Belmiro de Azevedo, John Bowmer, Peter Brabeck, Bill Burns, Patti Cazzato, Paul Dennehy, Rick Dobbis, Greg Dyke, Niall FitzGerald, David Gardner, Pete Goss, Simon Gulliford, Franz Humer, Margaret James, John Latham, Pat Lawless, Alain Levy, Paulanne Mancuso, Nigel Morris, Rob Murray, Ian Powell, David Prosser, Thomas Sattelberger, Sir Martin Sorrell, Jean Tomlin, and Karel Vuursteen.

We learned a great deal, too, from their close colleagues (followers, if you will) and from the organizations within which they—and often we—worked. These include Adecco, Barclays Bank, the BBC, Capital One, Chime, Electronic Arts, Gap, GlaxoSmithKline, Heineken, Legal & General, Lufthansa, Marks & Spencer, Nestlé, PolyGram, PWC, Roche, Rodborough School, SABMiller, Sonae, Sony Music, Unilever, and WPP.

Our students at London Business School, Insead, Henley Management College, and elsewhere provided a ready source of opinion and devil's advocates. Thanks in particular are due to our colleagues Estelle Bowman, Jay Conger, the late Sumantra Ghoshal, and John Hunt, all of whom provided advice, help, and encouragement along the way. Our agent Helen Rees once again helped us negotiate our way through the publishing world and we are grateful.

Practically, we would like to thank Caroline Madden for her helpfulness and patience with the manuscript and careful protection of our diaries so that, eventually, we finished the book.

At Harvard Business School Press, we were greatly helped by the patience, fortitude, and intellectual curiosity of Jeff Kehoe.

Successive editors of the *Harvard Business Review*—Suzy Wetlaufer and Tom Stewart—have encouraged our ideas, as have their editorial colleagues, in particular Diane Coutu. We are grateful for their continuing support. We are grateful, too, for the insights and editorial momentum provided by Stuart Crainer and Des Dearlove of Suntop Media.

Finally, thanks to our long-suffering families—Vickie, Shirley, Hannah, Tom, Rhian, Gemma, and Robbie—who have borne the costs of our often antisocial efforts to complete this book.

—Rob Goffee and Gareth Jones
London, June 2005

Introduction

1. All quotations in the book are from our research interviews unless otherwise attributed.

2. Robert D. Putnam, *Bowling Alone: The Collapse and Revival of American Community* (New York: Simon & Schuster, 2000).

3. Max Weber, *Economy and Society* (Cambridge, MA: Harvard University Press, 1954).

4. Alexis de Tocqueville, *Democracy in America* (Chicago: University of Chicago Press, 2000).

5. David Reisman, *The Lonely Crowd: A Study of the Changing American Character* (New Haven, CT: Yale University Press, 1961).

6. Putnam, *Bowling Alone*.

7. Richard Sennett, *The Corrosion of Character* (New York: W. W. Norton, 1998).

8. Michael B. Arthur and Denise M. Rousseau, eds., *The Boundaryless Career: A New Employment Principle for a New Organizational Era* (New York: Oxford University Press, 1996).

9. Richard Scase and Robert Goffee, *Reluctant Managers: Their Work and Lifestyles* (London: Unwin Hyman, 1989).

10. Max Weber, "Science as a Vocation," in *Max Weber: Essays in Sociology* (New York: Oxford University Press, 1975).

Chapter One

1. The literature adjacent to leadership—on motivation, teams, personal and organizational change, for example—is rich and interesting. But the leadership field narrowly defined is disappointing. Most standard textbooks in organizational behavior have an obligatory chapter on leadership. They usually conclude that effective leadership depends on the context. While we agree that it is fundamental

to accept that leadership is situational, it is disappointing that many accounts stop there, offering little help to individuals seeking to improve their own leadership. For a recent textbook review, see, for example, L. J. Mullins, *Management and Organizational Behavior,* 7th ed. (London: Financial Times Prentice Hall, 2004). For a masterly review of classic and recent leadership research, see Jay Conger and Rabindra N. Kanungo, *Charismatic Leadership in Organizations* (London: Sage, 1998).

2. Quoted material in this chapter was obtained from the following interviews: Bill Burns, interview by Rob Goffee, Barcelona 2002; Franz Humer, interview by Rob Goffee, Basel, February 2000.

3. We first developed this view in the article "Why Should Anyone Be Led by You?" *Harvard Business Review*, September–October 2000.

4. See in particular the work of Manfred Kets de Vries (see Diane Coutu, "Putting Leaders on the Couch," *Harvard Business Review,* January 2004), *The Leadership Mystique* (London: Financial Times Prentice Hall, 2002); and Michael Maccoby, "Narcissistic Leaders," *Harvard Business Review,* January–February 2000.

5. Mary Parker Follett, *Dynamic Administration* (New York: Harper, 1941); Fred Fiedler, *A Theory of Leadership Effectiveness* (New York: McGraw-Hill, 1967); Paul Hersey, *The Situational Leader* (Escondido, CA: Center for Leadership Studies, 1984); and Victor H. Vroom, "Situational Factors in Leadership," in *Organization 21C*, ed. Subir Chowdhury (London: Financial Times Prentice Hall, 2003).

6. The manner in which social reality is constructed is a major and influential strand of work within sociology, which has rarely been tapped for the purposes of leadership research and theory. For the classic account, see Peter L. Berger and Thomas Luckmann, *The Social Construction of Reality* (New York: Anchor Books, 1966).

7. The motivation literature on the significance of personal recognition and the appeal of challenging, stretching activities is most relevant. See, for example, John W. Hunt, *Managing People at Work* (London: McGraw-Hill, 1992).

8. The psychological literature is well summarized in Carl R. Rogers, *On Becoming a Person* (Gloucester, MA: Peter Smith Publisher, 1996); Robert Ornstein, *The Roots of the Self* (New York: HarperCollins, 1973); and Kenneth Gergen, *The Saturated Self* (New York: Basic Books, 1992).

9. The *Concise Oxford Dictionary* (Oxford: Oxford University Press, 1995).

10. Robert Dick and Tim Dalmau, *Values in Action: Applying the Ideas of Argyris and Schön* (Chapel Hill, Queensland, Australia: Interchange, 1990).

11. Jeffrey Pfeffer and Robert Sutton, *The Knowing-Doing Gap* (Boston: Harvard Business School Press, 1999).

12. Warren Bennis, *On Becoming a Leader* (Reading, MA: Addison-Wesley, 1989).

13. Seymour Martin Lipset and Reinhard Bendix, *Social Mobility in Industrial Society* (Somerset, NJ: Transaction Publishers, 1992); John H. Goldthorpe,

Social Mobility and Class Structure in Modern Britain (Oxford: Clarendon Press, 1980); Rosabeth Moss Kanter, *Men and Women of the Corporation* (New York: Basic Books, 1977).

14. Goffee and Jones, "Why Should Anyone Be Led by You?"

15. P. Christopher Earley and Elaine Mosakowski, "Cultural Intelligence," *Harvard Business Review,* October 2004.

16. Steven Lukes, ed., *Durkheim: The Rules of Sociological Method and Selected Texts on Sociology and Its Method* (London: Macmillan, 1982); and Emile Durkheim, *Suicide: A Study in Sociology* (Glencoe, IL: Free Press, 1951).

17. Georg Simmel, "Social Distance," in *The Sociology of Georg Simmel*, ed. Kurt H. Wolff (New York: Free Press, 1950); David Frisby, *Georg Simmel* (London: Tavistock, 1984).

18. This theme is apparent in the treatment of several significant historical and political leaders in John Adair's *Inspiring Leadership* (London: Thorogood, 2002).

19. Heike Bruch and Sumantra Ghoshal, "Management Is the Art of Doing and Getting Done," *Business Strategy Review*, Autumn 2004.

Chapter Two

1. Quotes in this chapter are from the following interviews, unless otherwise specified: Peter Brabeck, interview by Rob Goffee, Vevey, April 2003; Bill Burns, interview by Rob Goffee, Barcelona, December 2002; Rick Dobbis, interviews by Gareth Jones, New York and London, May 2003; Greg Dyke, interview by Gareth Jones and Rob Goffee, London, November 2002; David Gardner, interview by Rob Goffee, London, February 2003; John Latham, interview by Rob Goffee, Godalming, February 2003; Karen Marsh, interview by Rob Goffee, London Business School, May 2003; Sattelberger, interview by Rob Goffee, Frankfurt, September 2002; Martin Sorrell, interview by Rob Goffee, London, October 2002; Jean Tomlin, interview by Rob Goffee, London Business School, February, 2003

2. We discussed this theme in an earlier book: Richard Scase and Robert Goffee, *Reluctant Managers: Their Work and Lifestyles* (London: Unwin Hyman, 1989).

3. Issues of workplace change and identity are provocatively discussed in Richard Sennett's *The Corrosion of Character* (New York: W.W. Norton, 1998).

4. Carl R. Rogers, *On Becoming a Person* (Gloucester, MA: Peter Smith Publisher, 1996); Robert Ornstein, *The Roots of the Self* (New York: HarperCollins, 1973); and Kenneth Gergen, *The Saturated Self* (New York: Basic Books, 1992). Interestingly, a sociological perspective on these questions was opened up by George Herbert Mead in *Mind, Self and Society* (Chicago: University of Chicago, 1934), drawing on the work of Cooley. However, these early formulations were never really developed in the leadership literature. The links between narcissism and leadership are picked up in Michael Maccoby's and Manfred Kets de Vries's work.

5. Akio Morita, *Never Mind School Records* (Tokyo, Japan: Asahi Shimbun Publishing Company, 1987).

6. How leaders use their emotions to liberate the energies of others is discussed insightfully in Daniel Goleman, *Emotional Intelligence* (New York: Bantam, 1995).

7. Jim Collins, *Good to Great* (New York: HarperBusiness, 2001).

8. For a masterly discussion of identity, roles, and role distance, see the classic work by Erving Goffman, *The Presentation of Self in Everyday Life* (Gloucester, MA: Peter Smith Publisher, 1999).

9. Like Greg Dyke, Jean Tomlin has moved on since our interview. As we discuss in chapter 9, leadership inevitably exposes individuals to risks, including job loss.

10. See Manfred Kets de Vries (see Diane Coutu, "Putting Leaders on the Couch," *Harvard Business Review,* January 2004), *The Leadership Mystique* (London: Financial Times Prentice Hall, 2002); and Michael Maccoby, "Narcissistic Leaders," *Harvard Business Review,* January–February 2000.

11. Jay Conger and Rabindra N. Kanungo, *Charismatic Leadership in Organizations* (London: Sage, 1998).

12. Land and Jobs are discussed in Conger and Kanungo, *Charismatic Leadership*; Carlsson and Gyllenhammer, in Maccoby, "Narcissistic Leaders."

13. Contributions to the *Harvard Business Review* confirm the contemporary popularity of quiet leadership. See, for example, Joseph L. Badaracco, Jr., "We Don't Need Another Hero," *Harvard Business Review*, September 2001; James Collins, "Level 5 Leadership: The Triumph of Humility and Fierce Resolve," *Harvard Business Review*, January 2001; Debra Meyerson, "Radical Change, the Quiet Way," *Harvard Business Review*, October 2001.

14. David Kolb, *Experiential Learning* (London: Financial Times Prentice Hall, 1983).

15. For further discussion of cultural variation and identity, see Nancy J. Adler, *International Dimensions of Organizational Behavior*, 3rd ed. (Cincinnati, OH: Southwestern College Publishing, 1997); and P. Christopher Earley and Randall S. Peterson, "Elusive Cultural Chameleon: Cultural Intelligence as a New Approach to Intercultural Training for the Global Manager," *Academy of Management Learning and Education,* 2003.

16. C. Wright Mills, *The Sociological Imagination* (Oxford: Oxford University Press, 1990).

17. David Riesman, *The Lonely Crowd* (New Haven, CT: Yale University Press, 1973).

18. Ray Oldenburg, *The Great Good Place* (New York: Paragon House, 1991).

Chapter Three

1. Quotes in this chapter are from the following interviews, unless otherwise specified: Peter Brabeck, interview by Rob Goffee, Vevey, April 2003; Bill Burns, interview by Rob Goffee, Barcelona, December 2002; Greg Dyke, interview by

Gareth Jones and Rob Goffee, London, November 2002; Pete Goss, interview by Rob Goffee, London Business School, September 2002; Pauline Mancuso, interview by Rob Goffee and Gareth Jones, New York, February 2000; Paul McDermott, interview by Gareth Jones, London, March 2003.

2. *Foible* is defined in the *Concise Oxford Dictionary* as a minor weakness or idiosyncrasy. It is quite different from a fatal flaw.

3. In this sense, leadership is always instrumental; it is a relationship designed to achieve something. This distinguishes it from other types of relationship—friends or family, for example—that might be regarded as intrinsically good or desirable. The distinction is sometimes forgotten in contemporary discussions.

4. Alistair Mant, *Leaders We Deserve* (Oxford: Blackwell, 1983).

5. The story is told in his book, Greg Dyke, *Inside Story* (London: Harper-Collins, 2004).

6. Charles Taylor, *Sources of the Self* (Boston: Harvard University Press, 1989).

7. John W. Hunt, *Managing People at Work* (London: McGraw-Hill, 1992); and John Hunt, "The Leader as Exemplar," *Business Strategy Review*, 1997. See also John Viney's discussion of leadership, introversion, and distance in *Drive* (London: Bloomsbury, 1999).

8. Interesting insights on changing career structures can be found in Maury Peiperl et al., *Career Frontiers* (Oxford: Oxford University Press, 2000).

9. The phenomenon is not new; we discovered it initially in a survey of middle-level managers in the mid-1980s. See Richard Scase and Robert Goffee, *Reluctant Managers: Their Work and Lifestyles* (London: Unwin Hyman, 1989).

10. Studs Terkel, *Working* (London: Wildwood House, 1975).

11. The extent to which cultures allow the revelation of personal weakness without losing face will also be a constraining factor. The significance of face in Asian culture, for example, is important here. But it does not, in our view, totally preclude the leader from revealing humanizing weaknesses.

12. Simon Barnes, "Football Mourns Old Big 'Ead," *Times* (London), September 21, 2004.

13. Michael Parkinson, "Brian Clough," *Sunday Telegraph* (London), September 26, 2004.

14. Michael Parkinson, "He Was Loveable and Impossible, Wise and Silly. A Pickle of a Man," *Daily Telegraph* (London), September 21, 2004.

15. http://www.nottinghamforest.premiumtv.co.uk/

Chapter Four

1. Quotes in this chapter are from the following interviews, unless otherwise specified: John Bowmer, interview by Rob Goffee, London, October 2002; Bill Burns, interview by Rob Goffee, Barcelona, December 2002; Patti Cazzato, interview by Rob Goffee, San Francisco, November 2002; Greg Dyke, interview by Gareth Jones

and Rob Goffee, London, November 2002; John Latham, interview by Rob Goffee, Godalming, February 2003

2. See Daniel Goleman, *Emotional Intelligence* (New York: Bantam, 1995).

3. Daniel Goleman and Richard Boyatzis, *Primal Leadership* (Boston: Harvard Business School Press, 2002).

4. This notion is central to classical social theory as it emerged in the nineteenth century. The clearest expression is in the work of Emile Durkheim, who, in both *The Division of Labor in Society* (New York: Free Press, 1984) and Steven Lukes, ed., *Durkheim: The Rules of Sociological Method and Selected Texts on Sociology and Its Method* (London: Macmillan, 1982), insisted on society as a reality, *sui generis*—as a thing in itself. In the twentieth century, the work of Talcott Parsons insists on the understanding of the ends, means, and *conditions* of action. Both are in stark contrast to the naïve voluntarism of much leadership literature.

5. George Homans, *The Human Group* (London: Routledge and Keegan Paul, 1951).

6. Peter L. Berger and Thomas Luckmann, *The Social Construction of Reality* (New York: Anchor Books, 1966).

7. Although many leaders look as if they gather information on others almost naturally, our experience is that they build a rich picture of others through fairly systematic work. Our network analysis is designed as an aid in this process.

8. Summarized in most standard organizational behavior textbooks; see, for example, L. J. Mullins, *Management and Organizational Behavior,* 7th ed. (London: Financial Times Prentice Hall, 2004).

9. Jon Katzenbach and Douglas K. Smith, *The Wisdom of Teams* (Boston: Harvard Business School Press, 1992).

10. Randall Peterson and T. L. Simons, "Task Conflict and Relationship Conflict in Top Management Teams," *Journal of Applied Psychology,* 2000.

11. John W. Hunt, *Managing People at Work* (London: McGraw-Hill, 1992).

12. Deborah L. Duarte and Nancy Tennant Snyder, *Mastering Virtual Teams*, 2nd ed. (San Francisco: Jossey Bass, 2001).

13. Anthony Storr, *The Art of Psychotherapy* (London: Butterworth-Heinemann, 1990).

14. Tony Cockerill, "Ryder Cup Lessons in Team Play," *Business Strategy Review,* Winter 2004.

Chapter Five

1. Quotes in this chapter are from the following interviews, unless otherwise specified: Jean Tomlin interview by Rob Goffee February 2003; Dawn Austwick, interview by Rob Goffee, London, March 2004.

2. *Daily Telegraph* (London), November 17, 2004.

3. For an interesting discussion on the issues surrounding this topic, see "Clash of the Titans: When Top Executives Don't Get Along with the Team," Knowledge@Wharton.

4. Warren Bennis, "The Seven Ages of the Leader," *Harvard Business Review*, January 2004.

5. These concepts are embedded in the works of Emile Durkheim, Karl Marx, Max Weber, and Georg Simmel.

6. See Victor Vroom, *Work and Motivation* (New York: Wiley, 1954); R. D. Pritchard, "Organizational Productivity," in *Handbook of Industrial and Organizational Psychology*, 2nd ed., eds. Marvin D. Dunnette and Leaetta M. Hough (Palo Alto, CA: Consulting Psychologists Press, 1992).

7. George Homans, *The Human Group* (London: Routledge and Keegan Paul, 1951).

8. This is exemplified in, for example, the notion of strategic intent outlined by Gary Hamel and C. K. Prahalad in *Competing for the Future* (Boston: Harvard University Press, 1994).

9. The model is developed in Rob Goffee and Gareth Jones, *The Character of a Corporation*, 2nd ed. (London: Profile Books, 2003).

10. These and other historical examples are discussed in John Adair, *Inspiring Leadership* (London: Thorogood, 2002).

11. Pierre Bourdieu, *Distinction: A Social Critique of the Judgement of Taste* (Boston: Harvard University Press, 1984).

12. Warren Bennis, "The Seven Ages of the Leader," *Harvard Business Review*, January 2004.

Chapter Six

1. Quotes in this chapter are from the following interviews, unless otherwise specified: Bill Burns, interview by Rob Goffee, Barcelona, December 2002; Rick Dobbis, interviews by Gareth Jones, New York and London, May 2003; Nigel Morris, interview by Rob Goffee, Virginia, April 2003.

2. Georg Simmel, "Social Distance," in *The Sociology of Georg Simmel*, ed. Kurt H. Wolff (New York: Free Press, 1950); David Frisby, *Georg Simmel* (London: Tavistock, 1984).

3. Richard Sennett, *The Corrosion of Character* (New York: W. W. Norton, 1998).

4. Given our insistence that leadership is nonhierarchical, using formal position as a personal difference is a fatal error.

5. George Homans, *The Human Group* (London: Routledge and Keegan Paul, 1951).

6. John Adair, *Inspiring Leadership* (London: Thorogood, 2002).

7. Ibid.

8. John W. Hunt, *Managing People at Work* (London: McGraw-Hill, 1992).

9. This is precisely the effect that cognitive dissonance theory predicts. Cognitive dissonance arises when two or more behaviors, attitudes, feelings, or opinions are perceived as inconsistent. When this happens with leaders, their overall authenticity is brought into question.

10. Daniel Goleman, *Emotional Intelligence* (New York: Bantam, 1995).

11. In the United Kingdom, the Health and Safety Executive defines stress as "the adverse reaction people have to excessive pressure or other types of demand placed on them." In the United Kingdom, about half a million people experience work-related stress that they believe is making them ill. Up to five million people in the United Kingdom feel "very" or "extremely" stressed by their work. In the United States, almost one-third of the workforce feels overworked or overwhelmed by the amount of work they have to do.

12. In the United Kingdom, these are about the weather and the traffic. In the United States, they're about sports, and in the Netherlands, for some reason, they involve coffee.

13. Adair, *Inspiring Leadership*.

Chapter Seven

1. Quotes in this chapter are from the following interviews, unless otherwise specified: Peter Brabeck, interview by Rob Goffee, April 2003; Pete Goss, interview by Rob Goffee, London Business School, September 2002; Franz Humer, interview by Rob Goff, Basel, October 2002

2. Nancy Rothbard and Jay Conger, "Orit Gadiesh: Pride at Bain & Co. (A)," Case 9-494-031 (Boston: Harvard Business School, 1993).

3. Jay Conger, *Winning Them Over* (New York: Simon & Schuster, 1998).

4. Stephen Denning, "Telling Tales," *Harvard Business Review,* May 2004.

5. Sydney Finkelstein, "Seven Habits of Highly Ineffective Leaders," *Business Strategy Review*, Winter 2003.

6. Ibid.

7. Ibid.

8. Leslie A. Perlow and Stephanie Williams, "Is Silence Killing Your Company?" *Harvard Business Review*, May 2003.

9. Suzy Wetlaufer and Peter Brabeck, "The Business Case Against Revolution," *Harvard Business Review,* February 2001.

10. "Nestlé's Long-Term View," *Economist,* August 29, 2002.

11. John W. Hunt, *Managing People at Work* (London: McGraw-Hill, 1992).

12. Malcolm Gladwell, "The Perfect Chief Executive," *Times* (London), August 20, 2002.

13. Michael Hay and Peter Williamson, *The Handbook of Strategy* (Oxford: Blackwell, 1991).

14. Karl E. Weick and Diane L, Coutu, "Sense and Reliability: A Conversation with Celebrated Psychologist Karl E. Weick," *Harvard Business Review,* April 2003.

Chapter Eight

1. Loren Gary, "Neoteny: How Leaders Recruit the Right Kind of Followers," *Harvard Management Update,* September 2002; Robert E. Kelley, *The Power of Followership* (New York: Doubleday Currency, 1992).

2. Heike Bruch and Sumantra Ghoshal, "Managing Is the Art of Doing and Getting Done," *Business Strategy Review,* Autumn 2004.

3. Lynn Offerman, "When Followers Become Toxic," *Harvard Business Review*, January 2004.

4. Warren Bennis, *An Invented Life: Reflections on Leadership and Change* (Boulder, CO: Perseus Books, 1994).

5. E. P. Hollander, "Conformity, Status and Idiosyncrasy Credit," *Psychological Review* 65 (1958); and *Leaders, Groups, and Influence* (Oxford: Oxford University Press, 1964).

Chapter Nine

1. Greg Dyke, *Inside Story* (London: HarperCollins, 2004).

2. Ibid., 33

3. Ibid, 20–21.

4. Ibid., 25

5. Ibid., 25

6. Ibid.

7. Ibid.

8. Ibid.

9. David Hume, *Essays, Moral, Political, and Literary* (Indianapolis, IN: Liberty Classics, 1987).

10. Cited in Karl Popper, *In Search of a Better World* (London: Routledge, 1992).

11. John Adair, *Inspiring Leadership* (London: Thorogood, 2002).

ABOUT THE AUTHORS

Rob Goffee, is Professor of Organisational Behaviour at the London Business School. An internationally respected authority on organizational transformation, he has published ten books and more than fifty articles in scholarly and managerial journals. He is a frequent contributor to newspapers and magazines and has appeared as a guest on many radio and television programs on business issues. In addition, he consults with a number of large corporations on organizational change, corporate culture, board governance, and management development.

Gareth Jones, is a visiting professor at INSEAD and a Fellow of the Centre for Management Development at London Business School. He was Senior Vice President of Global Human Resources at Poly-Gram and, later, Director of Human Resources and Internal Communications at the BBC. His articles have appeared in the *European Management Journal*, *Human Relations*, and the *Harvard Business Review*. His research and consulting interests are in the areas of culture, leadership, and change.

Together, Goffee and Jones are the authors of "The Character of a Corporation" and the McKinsey prize-winning article "Why

Should Anyone Be Led by You?" published in the *Harvard Business Review*. They are the founding partners of Creative Management Associates, which has worked with some of the world's leading organizations on issues of corporate culture, organizational design, and leadership development.

Visit their Web sites at www.creative-management-associates .com and www.whyshouldanyonebeledbyyou.com.